W9-BZN-434

A TASTE *for* BEER

STEPHEN BEAUMONT

A TASTE *for* BEER

A Storey Publishing Book

STOREY

Storey Communications, Inc.
Schoolhouse Road
Pownal, Vermont 05261

The mission of Storey Communications is to serve our customers
by publishing practical information that encourages personal independence
in harmony with the environment.

Edited by Pamela Lappies
Cover design by Cynthia McFarland
Cover photograph by Nicholas Whitman
Text design and production by Kevin Connolly

Printed in Canada by Interglobe, Inc.
First Printing, August 1995

United States edition published in 1995 by Storey Communications, Inc., Schoolhouse Road, Pownal, Vermont 05261.

Canadian edition published in 1995 by Macmillan Canada, A Division of Canada Publishing Corporation, Toronto, Canada

Library of Congress Cataloging-in-Publication Data

Beaumont, Stephen, 1964–
   A taste for beer / Stephen Beaumont.
       p.   cm.
   "A Storey Publishing book."
   Includes bibliographical references.
   ISBN 0-88266-907-9 (pbk.)
   1. Beer.   2. Ale.   I. Title.
TP577.B36   1995
641.2'3—dc20
                                                95-11078
                                                   CIP

*Dedicated to my grandmother, Edna McNeill, and the memory of
my grandfather, Colonel William McNeill. Also to George and Elizabeth
Beaumont, who helped this book along in ways they will never know.*

TABLE OF CONTENTS

FOREWORD: A TASTE FOR BEER 1

THE RENAISSANCE BEGINS 4

GETTING TO KNOW YOUR BEER 16

    A Concise Catalogue of North American Beer Styles 28

ENJOYING LIFE WITH BEER 43

CELEBRATING THE SEASONS 63

    Spring 64

    Summer 68

    Fall 75

    Winter 81

A BEER AT THE TABLE 86

    Appetizers and Hors D'Oeuvres 90

    Soups and Salads 90

    Red Meats 92

    Poultry and Pork 94

    Fish 95

    Speaking of Heat 97

    Vegetarian Fare 98

The Tomato Issue   99

Barbecues   100

Brunch   101

Dessert   102

Cheese   103

Pleasing the Crowd   105

Beer Drinks   106

BEER IN THE KITCHEN   108

Soups and Salads   111

   Kielbasa, Cabbage and Ale Soup   111

   Gorgonzola Ale Soup   113

   Alberta Prairie Oysters   114

   Beer and Bean Soup   115

   Sunshine Citrus Salad   116

   Fourth of July Potato Salad   117

Sides, Snacks and Sauces   118

   Holy Cow! Neon Strips   119

   Cheese and Ale Spread   120

   Joe Fiorito's Baked Beans   121

   Shrimp and Chorizo Cheesecake on Black Bean Stout Sauce 123

   Baked Eggplant in Honey Beer   124

   Onion Rings with Beer and Rosemary   126

   Mushroom and Wheat Sauce   127

   Barbecued Stout Pasta Sauce   128

Breads   129

   Beer Focaccia   130

   Pumpkin Bread   131

Entrées   132

    Fettuccine with Weissbier Sauce   133

    Go Big Red Chili   134

    Boilermaker Jambalaya   135

    Mom's Ale Meat Loaf   137

    Moules à la Blanche (Mussels in White Beer)   139

    Pork and Yam Ragout with Caribbean Stout   140

    New Orleans Barbecue Shrimp   142

    Musk Ox Stroganoff   144

    Wendy's Waterzooï   145

    Pale Ale, Oyster and Potato Pie   147

    Wicked West Fajitas   149

Desserts   151

    Gingerbread Crust Pumpkin Pie   152

    Shake It Up   153

    Stout Cake   155

TO BOLDLY GO   156

APPENDIX I: THE BEERS OF THE BOOK   171

APPENDIX II: REFERENCES   177

A TASTE FOR
BEER

In 1985, the first three entrants in the new wave of what would come to be called microbreweries opened in Ontario. One brewed only lager, another just ale and the third offered one of each. Beer drinking would, for me, never again be the same.

I was in university then and, as students are wont to do, tended to drink a fair amount of beer. I was also living in a large Toronto house along with an ever-changing number of friends and housemates, so there was always someone around to remind me of the scholastic benefit of breaking off my studies in favor of going out for a beer, or so it seemed.

The brands that my friends and I carted home in those days were a mishmash of major brewery labels — Canadian, Crystal, Labatt's I.P.A., Carling O'Keefe's Carlsberg, Export, Grizzly, Molson Stock Ale. For although we each still harbored a small reserve of brand loyalty, we lingered under no illusion that one major brewery beer tasted significantly different from another; whim, price and force of habit, in that order, dictated most of our beer choices. Then came the opening of the micros.

I should mention here that in 1985, my friends and I were already predisposed toward beer that tasted different than the national brands. When we went to pubs, and could afford it, we drank German or Scottish lagers and English ales. At the government-run liquor stores, we bought from the very limited selection of imported beers such as Kronenbourg, Heineken and Newcastle Brown Ale when we wanted to treat ourselves. So when the micro brands finally hit the shelves, we were more than ready for them.

We still bought the major brewery labels with some frequency — we couldn't afford the higher-priced micros all the time! — but our attitude toward Canadian beer had shifted. After all, here were brands that tasted imported but were brewed within an hour's drive of Toronto or, in the case of one brewery, right downtown. It became harder and harder to convince ourselves of the merits of Molson, Labatt and Carling O'Keefe brands. Why, we asked for the first time, weren't their beers as tasty as those from the Brick, Upper Canada and Wellington County breweries?

The rest, as I am sure you know, is history. Those three breweries, and dozens like them across the continent, formed the vanguard of a new beer movement known diversely as craft brewing, microbrewing, artisanal brewing or the natural beer renaissance. They begat hundreds of others like them and, to this day, continue to change the way people think about beer. This book is, I believe, a logical extension of that ongoing process.

In the following pages, I plan to challenge every assumption you have ever made about beer, questioning some, refuting many and twisting others completely around. I will ask you why you don't drink beer with your dessert, question whether or not you have ever enjoyed a wheat beer with your Sunday-morning paper and make you wonder what beer style might best complement your favorite baseball team. And don't worry if answers to those questions don't immediately come to mind, because I'll be happy to help you out there, as well.

As you read and taste your way through this epistle to beer, you will find discussions of beer styles and their appropriateness to different occasions, a guide to matching beer with fine food and a look at some rather odd beery combinations, including a whimsical study of pairing beer with music. You will also find examples of how remarkably useful beer is in the kitchen and see how well beer can follow the changes in the seasons. And because this book is intended to help further the emerging beer culture on this continent, all of this will be related with a uniquely North American tone.

First and foremost, however, beyond all the stories and serving suggestions, this book is about the enjoyment of beer in all its forms. And not the "enjoyment" many North Americans *think* they get by drinking as much beer as they can on a weekend night, but the more tangible pleasures of discovering the rich silkiness of a well-made stout, the refreshing tang of a wheat beer or the quenching bite of a dry pilsner. These are the true pleasures of beer: the aromas, the complexities and the tastes.

In this increasingly hectic and pressure-filled world, the frantic pace at which we live can often seem like the dominant force in our existences. Faced with that kind of stress, we seek the occasional respite, however brief, from the daily grind—even a touch of pure hedonism now and then. If you can find that pleasure in a glass of good beer, then you will have found, as a friend of mind once put it, "a little bit of paradise."

★ ★ ★

No book like this can possibly be written without the assistance and co-operation of many people. In this case, those helpful souls number far too many for me to mention each and every one by name. I hope, therefore, that this overly generalized accounting will suffice and offer the observation that anyone who thinks that he or she deserves recognition here is likely correct, and I raise my glass to each of you.

My specific thanks go first to those men and women across North America who brew the beer we drink. Your help and patience — even when we have not seen eye-to-eye on what makes a beer great — is very much appreciated.

Thanks also to the publishers and editors of the numerous beer magazines and "brewspapers" for which I have written over the years, primarily *The Celebrator, All About Beer Magazine, Beer: the Magazine, BièreMAG, Beer Magazine* and *Southern Draft*. The latitude you have allowed me in writing for you has contributed significantly to the book you have before you. On the subject of editors, I also owe a great debt of appreciation to Nicole de Montbrun at Macmillan Canada, who helped me keep this project on track, and to Mario D'Eer and Lucy Saunders, who offered their very informed opinions on, respectively, the style and food matching chapters.

I cannot express enough gratitude to those beer writers who have come before me, including Fred Eckhardt, Alan Eames, Charlie Papazian and Jack Erickson. I must, however, single out Michael Jackson for special thanks. Indisputably the world's leading beer writer, Michael is the man who blazed the trails so many of us in this business are now following, and were it not for his hard work back in the lean days of the North American beer industry, I rather doubt this book would exist it its present form.

Finally, as always, I am very grateful for the support and assistance of my friends and family, especially my wife, Christine, who always believed that a person could make a living out of writing about beer, even when I doubted it myself.

Cheers!

CHAPTER 1

THE RENAISSANCE BEGINS

C ue lights and camera. The setting is a spectacular beach; white sand, palm trees visible in the distance, beautiful people playing volleyball in the background.

A blond-haired Adonis and his equally beautiful girlfriend walk into the frame, each holding a stalk of broccoli, and proceed to engage in numerous pleasure-filled beach activities. Action!

(**Voice-over**): This is it, folks, the vegetable with the taste that will stop you cold!

BROCCOLI!

It's the King of Vegetables! The one vegetable to have when you're having more than one! BROCCOLI tastes great, but is less filling! And you know that when you've said BROCCOLI, you've said it all!

You just can't miss with the green bullet, so when the day is done and you're ready to unwind, it's BROCCOLI TIME! Because when nothing else will do...

Tonight, let it be BROCCOLI!

The couple walk toward the camera, smile, kiss, take a nibble at each other's broccoli, turn and walk into the setting sun. Cut!

Have you caught that commercial on your television lately, perhaps sandwiched between the innings of a baseball game? Have you been carried away by the wave of broccoli-mania that is sweeping North America, making the noble floret the best-selling vegetable on the planet? Have you sacrificed all other legumes, tubers, fungi and assorted greens so that you might devote your diet exclusively to broccoli?

Of course, you haven't!

You haven't because there is no such advertisement, no such wave of broccoli-mania and absolutely no credibility to the notion that there ever could be, either. In fact, the very idea that such a phenomenon could occur stretches the limits of imagination well past the breaking point. Can you envision, for example, an ad campaign touting the "lifestyle-benefits" of broccoli? Or a marketing scheme aimed at persuading North Americans to forsake all other vegetables in deference to broccoli. Or a related industry built around T-shirts, baseball caps, athletic wear, designer shorts, denim jackets, watches and fashion accessories of every description, all emblazoned with stylized depictions of broccoli and slogans promoting its consumption?

It's a crazy concept, to be sure, one scarcely deserving of consideration. So why is a beer book engaging in such a fanciful analysis of broccoli marketing? Because, as ludicrous as the above scenario appears when applied to a vegetable, it is a very real and sound strategy in North America when it comes to beer.

STYLE VS. SUBSTANCE

This continent is home to a multimillion-dollar advertising industry devoted exclusively to the art of persuading beer drinkers to stick to a single, specific brand of beer. And the agencies that make up this industry work in exactly the same way as our fictional broccoli marketer: ignore the taste (taste doesn't matter); sell the image (bigger, bolder, fresher, drier ...); market the idea that "X" brand of beer will help make the consumer a better (stronger, more popular, sexier, more beautiful...) person and repeat the message as often as possible.

As an argument in favor of a product, it's lunacy. As a sales and marketing strategy, it's one of the most successful in history.

It is so successful that over forty percent of all the beer sold in the United States comes from a single brewing company—Anheuser-Busch! It is so successful that over ninety percent of all the beer sold in Canada comes from two brewing companies—Molson and Labatt! It is so successful that the over five hundred craft breweries operating in North America at the time of writing barely make a dent in the continent's total beer market!

It is so successful that it has convinced the vast majority of North Americans that beer is "just beer."

But beer is more than "just beer." Beer is the smoky richness of a porter and the crisp bitterness of a pilsner. It is the warming depth of a doppelbock and the fruity tang of a wheat beer, the reflective complexity of a barley wine and the foresty charm of a best bitter. Beer is a quenching drink, a soothing elixir and an invigorating tonic. And still, beer is so very much more.

Fortunately, just as it looked as though the advertising forces and mass commercial brewers would get their way and beer in North America would forever be little more than a generic product, a new generation of microbrewers or craft brewers or artisanal brewers, whatever you wish to call them, came to life sometime in the early to mid-1980s in response to the tiny but resilient demand for beer with taste. Guided more often than not by the dream of one or two dedicated, beer-loving businessmen, these microbreweries harked back to a time when brewing companies were local businesses producing beer for local people.

They were a feisty lot, these brewing revivalists, and they took the small audience they had for their beer and cultivated it with almost evangelical fervor into a legitimate market force. If they did not exactly save beer *per se*, they certainly rescued its flavor.

The craft beer renaissance has taken place in various stages over the course of the past couple of decades, with the most activity occurring over the last five years, and it has spawned hundreds upon hundreds of breweries, ranging in size from impossibly small to merely tiny. (Or, at least, that's the way they appear relative to brewing giants like Miller, Coors, Molson, Labatt and the biggest of them all, Anheuser-Busch.)

In turn, the brewers at these small breweries, often working with more vision and heart and love of brewing than commercial concern, have gifted the continent with thousands of brands covering virtually the entire spectrum of style and flavor. They have sweated and toiled to bring us wheat beers full of banana and clove notes, ales blessed with floral aromas and delicious earthy complexities of taste, light ales flavored with herbs, spices and fruits of almost every imaginable description and rich, warming and fortifying strong ales and bocks. And many beer lovers have responded with gratitude and a newfound recognition of the remarkable diversity that exists within that simple classification of beer.

Of course, acceptance of these new brews has not exactly been unanimous. The continental recognition of beer's incredible diversity of color, aroma and taste has been slow to come about, and to a great degree it is still in its early development. But where before there was only "beer," there now stand stouts and bocks and pilsners and ales of all types. People's tastes have changed and are continuing to change and it is at this point, this transition of taste, that this book truly begins.

GETTING USED TO FLAVOR

While it is one thing to discover new delights of the palate, it is quite another to figure out what to do with them. After all, if you have recently stumbled upon the joy of raw oysters on the half shell, you do not immediately start serving them to your family for breakfast. Similarly, when you discover what a treat a strong and forceful ale can be, you would be well advised not to take a case to a sunny July barbecue. No, like most gastronomic glories, beer has a schedule all its own. There are times when an ebony stout would be more appropriate than your favorite ale, other occasions when a lighter wheat beer would suit and still other instances when that fave ale would be just about the best taste possible.

Over the course of the last two or three decades, North Americans have learned what the French and the Italians have known for centuries, namely that wine only gets better with the addition of the perfect meal or great company. Now it is time that we also accept what the Belgians and Germans have taken as fact for countless generations — that beer likewise improves with the right social or gastronomic accompaniment.

In the following pages, you will be introduced to a tremendous variety of beers, from sublime gems like Creemore Springs Premium Lager to such outrageous, hop-suffused extremes as Rogue's Doppel Mogul Ale. And at each stop, you will find an occasion or a food that will suit these brews to a tee, for no matter how good a beer may be intrinsically, there exists no brew on the face of the planet that cannot be improved with the felicitous addition of environment, food or good company.

But as much as this book is about beer, it is also about something else, a less definable topic but one of at least equal importance: the reclamation of enjoyment.

When I first conceived of this book, I saw it as a tribute to the many ways in which beer may be enjoyed, savored and relished. As the project developed, however, I realized that I was on to something greater than merely a homage to beer. What I was unwittingly developing was a manifesto for the appreciation of life and all it offers us. The means was still beer, but the message was to stop and smell the hops.

ENJOYING VS. DRINKING

Enjoyment — true enjoyment — is a term that has almost lost its meaning as we hurtle toward the twenty-first century. Like such words as *fantastic* and *unique*, the frequent and random use of the word *enjoyment* has diluted its impact to the point that we frequently say we "enjoy" things which, were we to be perfectly honest, we only marginally more than tolerate. Glorious and unchecked enjoyment is fast becoming as rare as a soft breeze on a sweltering August night or a juicy, perfectly formed peach.

What I wish to present to you here, then, is a celebration of enjoyment, of indulgence, of pleasure. Of course, I will speak of beers — this is a beer book, after all — but also of tables stacked high with ebony breads, spiced and smoky meats, clementines filled to bursting with nature's nectar and roasted nuts of all descriptions; or tender tamales, sweet and sticky *frijoles*, irresistibly mouth-searing peppers and succulent fried plantains; or *al dente* pastas, fragrant and velvety olive oils, juicy, herb-laden sausages and clay-baked garlic.

Not that this journey into enjoyment will stop at the table, for pleasure comes in many forms: the thrill of music as played with the kind of vitality that comes only from a musician openly reveling in its performance; or the glory of a sun-drenched afternoon when one's sole concern is how best to extend the day's lazy pleasures into the night; or the unique feeling of warmth that stems from time well spent with lifelong friends. These joys, and many others, will be explored in the following pages.

One reason, if not *the* reason, we have lost touch with enjoyment is the way in which our high-tech, fast-paced world has developed its unnatural emphasis on speed and efficiency. We race from home to office to lunch and back to the office and, finally, home again. Our food is fast, our beverages "lite" and our entertainment facile. We can transmit a document around the globe in a matter of minutes but we can't find the time for a leisurely lunch accompanied by a good glass of beer.

It is indeed ironic that we spend so much time making money yet deny ourselves the opportunity to enjoy that which we earn. And when we are questioned about this, we answer with the familiar complaints about not having enough time and, even if we did, surely such indulgences are strictly the domain of the playful rich. But how much time or money do we need in order to revel in the taste of an exquisite beer? Twenty minutes? Three or four dollars? Enjoyment is not only within our grasp, it is already in our daily lives. We simply don't recognize it.

It really does not take much. An hour a day — half that, even — spent relaxing with a good book, a splendid piece of music or a great beer, savoring life rather than living it full-throttle, appreciating instead of merely noticing, and sipping rather than gulping. Call it spiritual time, a rest break or a mental-health moment, such pauses in life, whether with a beer or without, are among the best remedies we can take for the stress of our day-to-day lives, and they do not require a prescription, either. It is the truly busy person who cannot find time for such short respites and the astoundingly well-tempered individual who cannot benefit from them.

The bottom line of this epistle to beer, then, is that you revel in your own existence for at least a few moments each day. As ever, my position remains that life is far easier to live fully than we are led to believe by the trendsetting gurus of our modern age. You don't need a lot of money or even excessive amounts of time, just a palate and the will to spend some time on yourself. It may cut against the teachings of the advertisers, culture cops and spin doctors, but who cares what they think, anyway?

THE BOOK OF BEER ENJOYMENT

As anybody committed to their work knows, it is very easy to get caught up in one's job and lose perspective on what it is you do. Talk to someone in the plumbing trade and you will hear how disgracefully people treat their pipes; engage in a conversation with a dentist and the subject will center on how dental hygiene will better your life; a musician will tell you how she is going to change the world through her lyrics; and someone from the food processing industry will tell you how his new cryogenic freezing process will revolutionize life on earth. And so it is with the beer industry.

Over the years, I have spoken with many people associated with the beer industry, from casual aficionados to brewery presidents, and most of them are genuinely pleasant people with a good sense of humor and feet firmly planted on the ground. To talk to some, however, is to get the impression that the sky is falling and their favorite beer is the only thing that will keep it up! For them, beer is more than a drink, it is an evangelical pursuit.

Which is fine. Good food and drink should fire our passions and invigorate our sense of self, and the fervor with which some people approach beer is merely a reflection of those qualities. When the passion and bombast is set aside, however, two very simple facts quickly become apparent: first, beer is a thoroughly enjoyable beverage that, when treated with respect, can offer a great deal of pleasure to both the avid and occasional consumer, and second, the more you know about beer, the more enjoyment it can offer. These two truths form the cornerstone of this book.

There are numerous books on the market devoted to the pursuit of beer in its many manifestations and at least an equal number dedicated to home brewing. There are excellent cookbooks that will instruct you on how to prepare marvelous meals with beer and a host of fine regional, national and international guides to show you where to find different beers. Other books, or parts of books, will teach you the proper way to taste and judge beer and still others will dwell on the noble history of the brewing arts. The book you hold in your hands is none of these, although aspects of all of them will creep into the text now and again.

This is a book about beer enjoyment in all of its forms and, because of that sweeping mandate, certain generalizations have been made lest it become encyclopedic in volume. For example, readers well acquainted with the brewing arts will note the lack of detail in the brief description I give of the brewing process and the severe restrictions I place on the specifics offered in the style section. In my own defense, I can only note that I have simplified these issues because I believe them to be of relatively minor importance to the individual in pursuit of pure, unpretentious beer pleasure.

TRISTAN, THE MICROBREWERY DOG

In the summer of 1994, my friends Geoff and Kim bought a purebred shelty puppy and named him Tristan. Like most young dogs, Tristan was a rambunctious pup and enjoyed playing, running in circles and tugging on bones, chew-toys, clothing and virtually anything else he could get his tiny teeth into.

When my wife, Christine, and I went to visit Tristan for the first time, we thought it fitting to bring a gift and so I stuck in my pocket a hot dog-shaped chew-toy that had been given to me as part of Molson's launch of their Red Dog brand of beer. As puppies usually love to gnaw on things, I thought that the present would be suitable. What I didn't anticipate was Tristan's reaction.

Rather than greedily sinking his teeth into the rawhide hot dog, Tristan ran around the toy barking hysterically. His general pattern was to circle the bone several times, barking all the while, then pounce on it, pull back almost immediately and begin the process again. This dog had a serious problem with this toy!

We thought Tristan's behavior odd, but really didn't think much of it until, several months later, Geoff told me about his furry friend's drinking habits. It seemed that when Geoff would pour Tristan a little microbrewed beer — as dog owners are wont to do — his pup would eagerly lap it up. But when Geoff's in-laws tried to serve up a spot of Labatt's Blue to Tristan, he just turned up his snout at it! With no coaching at all, this diminutive canine connoisseur knew to favor full-flavored, craft-brewed beer over commercially oriented lagers.

From this behavior, we deduced that Tristan had known that the hot dog chew-toy came from Molson and thus reacted in an appropriate manner for a dog of his refined taste. This was a puppy who not only knew what he liked but would not tolerate even the presence of products from breweries he didn't like.

First and foremost, this is a consumer's book. Its intent is not to indoctrinate its audience into the growing fraternity of self-described "beer geeks," but to encourage everyone in the moderate, yet unrestrained, enjoyment of beer. My goal is to get you, the reader, basking in the gastronomic glories of beer, whether it be at the dinner table, at the ballpark or on the patio of your favorite bar or brewpub. And if, on occasion, I climb up on my soapbox in praise of beer, I hope you will forgive me my digressions and omissions and chalk it up to the passion I feel for this fine beverage.

THE CRITIC'S ROLE

One of the mine fields one must negotiate when writing a book about beer is that people inevitably wish to know which specific brews you like and which ones you dislike. And once they know that, they want to know which ones you merely like and which ones you LOVE.

In *Glutton for Punishment*, an autobiographical account of his days as restaurant reviewer for *Gourmet* magazine, Jay Jacobs rightly observes that readers are quite willing to follow — by rote — recommendations that are substantiated only by their existence in print. "If the disproportionate impact of favorable ink is somewhat alarming, it's at least understandable," he writes, "[because] presumably, readers are on the lookout for worthwhile experiences they may have missed."

Naturally, there is nothing wrong with this type of reader reaction and, in truth, it is part of what makes being a critic worthwhile. To laud a great product and have it well received by the public is one of the critic's finest rewards. I still remember my first full-blown published rave, like a first kiss, and the astounding reaction that followed it.

The beer was the 1990 Eisbock from Niagara Falls Brewing, a truly spectacular beer from what was then a very young brewery. I thought, and still think, that it was one of the greatest brews seen in years in Canada and I wrote as much in *The Toronto Star*, a newspaper with a Saturday circulation of about two million. Some time later, I spoke with the head of the small Niagara brewing company and he informed me that the response to my story was far greater than I ever would have imagined possible. People were telephoning the brewery long distance to reserve cases of the bock — no small expense at six dollars per 750mL bottle — and driving three or four hours to purchase their bottles. It was a heady revelation, and to this day, I still believe that I played a role, albeit a small one, in the success of this magnificent beer.

For every positive, however, there is a negative, and the less enthusiastic pronouncements I have foisted upon certain brews have brought their own consequences. I have had brewers and beer lovers attack my judgment because it did not coincide with theirs; I even know of one industry personality who, to this day, dislikes me because I do not find each and every one of his brands to be among the best in the world — despite the praise I have awarded certain of his company's brews.

In truth, I have never been completely comfortable with this element of beer criticism. To take someone's work, over which they have toiled endless hours, and reduce it to two or three sentences commands a sizable degree of responsibility, and to be critical of a beer that I perceive to be in some way flawed is an even greater burden.

If the beer is inspiring, the grandiose adjectives may flow in a torrent of praise and everyone can feel happy and proud of the review. If, however, the beer is mediocre, the consumer has a right to know and the reviewer an obligation to report the facts, but that does not mean that the brewer has any less pride in his or her work or will be any less hurt by a negative write-up. And most important, it does not change the fact that the review is but one man's opinion.

You see, it's a tricky business, even without mentioning the fans of a particular brewer's work who will be outraged if the beers they love garner anything less than glowing appraisals. Or the danger that something went awry with one and only one batch of the rated brew, and that just happened to be the batch that was sampled for review. Or, and this is worst of all, the chance that, out of necessity, the beer was sampled at a bad time for the reviewer and was thus subjected to the vagaries of the critic's mood or palate fatigue.

To combat these difficulties as best I can, I have tried through the years to duplicate tasting whenever possible and emphasize descriptions of the beers I review rather than subjective judgments. The theory behind this is that, although my assessment of a beer's ultimate worth may differ from that of a reader, a description will provide the reader with the tools necessary to make his or her own determination. It seemed like a good idea to me but, as I have found, it neglects the very element that leads people to seek the work of a professional critic: guidance. As I continued my work, however, I found that this guidance can take many forms.

WHAT FORM?

This book is not a beer guide and neither does it presume to be one; it does not contain extensive reviews of North American beers nor does it catalogue all the worthy brews produced on this continent. It is meant not to guide you to specific brands but, rather, to illustrate the numerous ways in which beer may contribute to the quality of your life. If I suggest anything that might influence your beer-buying habits, it is that you experiment with beers of all sorts, all brands and all styles.

Having noted that, I will now add that the beers mentioned in this book are, for the most part, beers that I have tasted and enjoyed. They represent good, very good or even excellent examples of the brewer's art and illustrate well their respective styles. Should you wish to look for any specific beer, it will be referenced in Appendix I, but will not be marked, rated or otherwise quantified in any way.

WHAT BEERS?

As much as I would have liked to, I have not tasted every beer in North America. To do so would certainly require a life lived constantly on the road and even then, the amazing growth of craft brewing in North America is such that a person could never catch up. So instead of attempting the impossible, I have, over recent years, compiled an extensive private listing of reviews of beers from several hundred breweries.

No doubt there will be numerous great beers that merit inclusion but which, for one reason or another, I have missed. At the time of writing, for example, there are reportedly dozens of brewpubs and breweries entering the start-up phase in New Jersey alone and numerous others that have sprung up in the Canadian prairies since my last visit, and all of these will be absent from this book because of nothing more than time limitations. To those owners and brewers whom I have missed, I can only apologize, and to the beer-loving reader, I will reemphasize the importance of trying a wide variety of the beers available in your area. Please remember that it is only through trial and experimentation that you can determine your own personal likes and dislikes.

On the subject of beer inclusion or the lack thereof, a studious reader may notice the underrepresentation of beers from Mexico and the Caribbean. This omission has occurred not through neglect, but because, even after repeated evaluations, I have not found many of the brews from these regions to be inspirational.

While the microbrewing renaissance has been in full flight in Canada and the United States, it has remained an unknown quantity in Mexico and the Caribbean and this has resulted in a continuation of the exclusivity that such breweries as Cuauhtémoc, Modelo, Moctezuma, Banks, and Desnoes and Geddes enjoy in those areas. And although a few of the beers produced by those companies range from good to very good in quality, brands like Dos Equis, Dragon Stout and Bohemia represent the exception rather than the rule in Mexican and Caribbean brewing.

BEWARE THE HOP-HEAD

Aby-product of the craft brewing renaissance has been the rise of a species of impassioned, beer-tasting humanoids known as the hop-heads.

The evolution of the hop-head has been closely linked to the hop-deprivation forced upon North Americans for years by the big breweries and it has been conjectured that the species arose in direct response to that environment. Although they come in all shapes and sizes and are virtually indiscernible from humans, hop-heads are characterized by one major, unalterable trait: an overriding adoration of anything hoppy. Among the negative character traits shown by hop-heads are the outright dismissal of non-hoppy beers regardless of their relative quality, the prejudiced view that all lagers are inherently bad or, at least, of a lesser class than ales and the automatic acceptance of all hoppy ales regardless of balance or quality.

There is growing speculation that the hop-head may be not a new species but a mutation of *Homo sapiens*. Preliminary evidence demonstrates that when a major-brand beer drinker is fed microbrewery products, particularly those of northern California, the Pacific Northwest and Quebec, the subject will begin showing hop-head traits, usually within a month or two. This is a fate to be avoided by all beer drinkers as it seriously warps a person's perception of beer. If you believe that you or a friend or family member is in danger of becoming a hop-head, please contact your closest beer expert, journalist or brewer immediately.

ONE LAST NOTE BEFORE WE START

One of the strange paradoxes that affect human existence is that most things that give us pleasure also carry the potential to do us harm. This is true of virtually anything from which we derive pleasure, from jogging to eating to drinking to relaxing. Everything is poison to our bodies; it is only a matter of degree.

If we bask in too much sun, for example, we risk skin cancer; too much sugar or fat and we become obese; excessive amounts of rest at the expense of exercise and our bodily functions will slowly grind to a halt; and too much exercise at the expense of rest and our muscles will tear and ligaments snap. In this same vein, too much beer will bring about numerous negative health effects.

Most experts agree that, consumed in moderate amounts, beer will cause people no harm and may even have positive health implications. We know, for example, that beer is an excellent source of carbohydrates and that brewer's yeast—the kind found in health food stores and unfiltered beers—is rich in complex B vitamins. But these benefits are *only* realized when beer is consumed in moderation.

For some reason, however, humans are not noted for being exceptional proponents of moderation. We spend years being told by our parents how bad it is to be drunk, and then we rush to try out drunkenness for ourselves as soon as the opportunity presents itself. Subsequently, as if to rationalize our actions, we convince ourselves that getting and being drunk is in some bizarre way enjoyable. All told, it is very strange behavior, indeed.

(It is also, it should be added, a strong case for the elimination of legal drinking ages. It seems apparent to me, at least, that children raised with beer would have less curiosity about it than those raised to regard beer as "forbidden fruit." This familiarity with beer, learned in the home under parental supervision, would then make the child less likely to rush out to experiment with excess and more likely to develop a respectful appreciation for alcohol later in life. As I was raised in a home where I was allowed to drink small amounts of beer and wine at an early age, I am a strong adherent to and proponent of this philosophy.)

Anyone who is being honest with him- or herself will readily admit that being drunk is not really all that much fun, and that the next morning is even less so. But we do it anyway and promise ourselves that it was definitely the last time—until next time, that is—and swear off all alcohol, even beer, for a few days or a few weeks.

Alcohol, however, is not the problem; *the excessive consumption of alcohol is the problem.* Thus, by swearing off our beer with dinner or our after-work pint, we are not solving the problem at all and, in fact, may be compounding it by creating a great thirst for that "forbidden fruit" when our beer fast comes to an end. A far better cure for drunkenness, it would seem, would be to develop a responsible admiration of the qualities of beer and an appreciation of how it can enhance our daily lives. One or two beers at dinner, seven nights a week, certainly would appear to be better for you than fourteen in one night!

So appreciate the fine work that the brewers of North America have done to bring you the beers mentioned in the pages of this book. Admire these brews for the depth of their aroma and the brilliance of their color. Relish the luxuries of their flavors and the spectacular ways in which they contribute to the enjoyment of so many occasions. And most of all, celebrate them for what they truly are: drinkable works of art.

CHAPTER 2

GETTING
TO KNOW YOUR
BEER

W hat is your favorite beer?"
It's a question that anyone who writes regularly about beer is bound to hear repeatedly, and to the casual beer drinker, it makes perfect sense. This is because that casual beer drinker—let's call him Irv—has a favorite beer that he normally drinks, as well as a few back-up brands for when Beer #1 is unavailable. Irv thinks that this is the most natural thing in the world because all of his friends have "their own" brands, his father and grandfather each drank a signature brand all of their lives and media advertising constantly reinforces in his mind the idea that a favorite beer is something you find and stick with for the rest of your days.

This philosophy works well for old Irv and if he sticks with it long enough, he will move one step further and declare that any beer that does not taste like "his beer" isn't really beer at all. Porters, barley wines, extra special bitters and wheats will all taste "funny" and Irv will dismiss them with a wave and go back to his glass of big-brewery beer.

But Irv is only cheating himself, because he's missing out on the world of color, aroma, body and, of course, taste available to the adventurous beer drinker. From refreshingly tart wheats to sweet and cloying old ales, bitter and quenching pilsners to satisfying and invigorating stouts, and dry and woody pale ales to sweet and flavorful fruit beers, the range of characters in these brews, and the dozens of other styles and the thousands of variations within them, is truly awe-inspiring. There is, indeed, a beer for every occasion.

To pick a favorite from among the fantastic array of beers brewed around the globe would be tantamount to trying to decide on a favorite selection from the world of music. How could anyone possibly be expected to choose between, say, Leonard Bernstein conducting the New York Philharmonic in Tchaikovsky's *Romeo and Juliet*, Louis Armstrong leading his orchestra in *Basin Street Blues* or John Lee Hooker playing it solo on *Crawling King Snake*? To describe one of these great pieces as being superior to the other two would require weighing such factors as the time of the day, the setting and the listener's current mood. And then to pick one and only one to be the sole selection on the jukebox forever... well, I think you get the idea.

The point is that different beers lend themselves equally well to different occasions. Just as you may not relish the thought of dance music first thing in the morning, you may likewise balk at the prospect of a rich oatmeal stout at a mid-June picnic lunch. But change the setting and circumstances to a Friday night, and the dance music, and maybe the stout, as well, becomes immediately more palatable. Similarly, grilled trout for breakfast is about as enticing as cold wheat beer on a freezing January night, but alter the time and mood to a sunny summer backyard barbecue and each offering becomes positively mouth-watering.

There was a time, not too long ago, when it didn't really matter what North American beer you drank because they all tasted more or less the same. Sure, there was the odd dark, malty lager or moderately hoppy ale, but with only forty to fifty breweries to choose from continent-wide, the selection was not exactly what you might call great.

Time has changed that dreary picture, however, and what was a beer wasteland has now blossomed into a bountiful garden of beer choices. As of early 1995, the number of North American breweries had skyrocketed to more than 600 and the variety of beer has increased proportionately, with no sign of this growth being stemmed. Where there were once lagers, lagers and more lagers, there are now dozens upon dozens of beer styles, some of which, like the myriad spiced and fruit beers that now populate the beerscape, would scarcely have been imaginable in the late 1970s.

Such an explosion of selection is without question a miraculous thing for long-suffering North American beer aficionados, but it also brings with it a degree of confusion for beer drinkers unfamiliar with such variety. After all, just as a person raised on meat and potatoes is unlikely to convert to Mediterranean fare upon his first taste, a beer drinker who is scarcely familiar with anything outside of light lager can hardly be expected to immediately embrace a clove-accented hefe-weizen or a coffee-dominated porter.

But clove and coffee are just two of the massive catalogue of diverse tastes that may now be found in North American beers, and two of the more conventional ones at that. Today's brews are apt to hold a vast range of tastes, some of which we traditionally associate with beers and others that just seem too off-the-wall to be real. For example, how about a chocolate or licorice stout? Or a brown ale touched with nuances of banana? And how does a grassy lager or an appley ale sound? What about a bock with soft notes of tomato? And these are just a few of the flavors that end up in beer through normal brewing methods, *without the addition of fruit or spice!*

If all of this seems too bizarre to imagine, fear not. Even experienced beer drinkers — those with experience drinking *different* types of beer, not large quantities of it — sometimes pale at the thought of some of the fruits, vegetables and spices that we tasters find in beer. To understand how these flavors end up in your glass, it will help to take a quick look at the brewing process before we launch into the basics of beer taste and the fundamentals of beer style.

BREWING BEER

Making beer is easy. All you need do is steep some malted barley until the grain releases its sugars into the water, run the sugary liquid into a kettle and boil it along with some hops, filter the resultant mixture into another container and allow it to cool, add some yeast, wait a week or two and you will have made beer. Now, making *good* beer... well, that is a completely different matter.

You begin with the first and most plentiful ingredient, water. Now, water might seem like a simple enough ingredient — turn on the kitchen tap and it flows like, well, like water. But that water likely has chlorine added to it at the municipal treatment plant, and you don't want that in your beer, so you must either filter your brewing water or find a pure spring source that can supply for your needs. Merely a minor issue, right? One that is easily solved, right? Wrong.

Even fresh, pure springwater may not be automatically suited to brewing. This is because such matters as mineral content and alkalinity (pH level) may not be correct for the style of beer you wish to brew. Adjustments may have to be made, minerals added or filtered out and, even then, you still have to factor in how your water will react with your brewing ingredients. For although water's role in brewing is often ignored by beer aficionados, it does make up some 90–95 percent of the finished brew and, as such, will affect the final taste of a beer. But let's say that you have managed to figure out your water. The next step is to select your malt.

If water is the base upon which your beer is built, then barley malt is your building material. The malting process, which dates back millennia, is accomplished by soaking the barley until it begins to germinate and then kilning it so that the sprouting of the grain is halted. The purpose of this teasing growth is to persuade the barley grains to free up important starches that will later be converted to fermentable sugars in the mash. And just as you would be picky about your bricks if you were building a house, so should you be picky about your barley when you are making beer.

First, you must decide whether you want to use exclusively the traditional two-row variety of barley or add a portion of the huskier six-row type. Then you have to choose your maltster—the company that will provide the malt you have chosen—often having nothing more upon which to base your decision than reputation and availability. But if you do your homework, you should be able to assure yourself of a reasonable quality of barley malt.

Now you must decide what types of malt you wish to use and how much you want of each. Mind, now, that this is different than the decision you made in the preceding step; there you were choosing barley types, while here you are selecting how you wish your malt kilned and the degree to which you may or may not want your malt or malts roasted after kilning. The range available runs the gamut from the basic pale malts with their sweet, slightly toasty grain tastes all the way to the deep, dark and rich chocolate and black malts, and each of these will contribute a different group of flavors and colors to your beer. Of course, you must be careful how you mix and match your grains, for the malts will react with each other to produce a whole medley of tastes. This is also the stage at which you must decide if you wish to use grains such as wheat, rice, corn or even rye, not to mention any other additives like liquid, crystal or cane sugar, or corn syrup.

On to the boil! Here the choices start to become rather complex—*as if they have been simple up to now*! First, you must select from among the dozens of domestic and imported hops available in North America. You may want some bittering hops to be added during the initial and middle stages of the boil and you will need some aroma hops that will be tossed in near the end. Once you have selected the varieties of hops you wish— did I mention that you also have to choose between leaf or pelletized hops?—you have to decide when each type will enter the boil and how much will be used.

Each of your hop decisions is going to profoundly affect the final character of your beer in the same way that the herbs and spices you choose, and when you elect to use them, will affect the taste of any dish you cook. Characteristics from bitterness to woodiness and flavors from nuts to grapefruit will all be determined by your hopping choices. And while you are making these decisions, you should make up your mind as to whether you want to add other flavor-enhancing substances such as herbs, spices, fruit or even citrus rinds. In today's brewing, almost anything goes and your limits will only be defined by you.

After boiling up all these ingredients for exactly the right amount of time, the wort—that's the brewing term for this sugary, hoppy soup you have made—will have to be cooled and filtered. That accomplished, you need only add your yeast.

But what yeast will you use? There are ale yeasts and lager yeasts, but that is only the beginning. Each individual strain and strain mutation will impart its own characteristics to the finished brew, so all your work to this point may be in vain if you do not use the perfect yeast. That one will make your ale taste rather banana-like while this one will contribute a spicy flavor and that other one will make your brew highly carbonic. Once again, do your homework and you should be all right, but a little praying wouldn't hurt, either.

Once the yeast has finished working its magic, you have a few more basic choices to make. Do you wish to dry-hop it, that is, add more hops to contribute a drier, leafier character? Will you carbonate using priming sugar, by krausening (reinvigorating the yeast through the addition of a small amount of unfermented wort) or simple CO_2 injection? Do you wish to opt for bottle- or cask-conditioning? How long will you age your beer? Do you pasteurize or filter your beer, or serve it unfiltered? The decision-making process does not stop until the customer is actually drinking your beer.

If you have successfully avoided all the perils and potholes that the brewing arts throw in your path, you should have made a good beer. But have you made exactly what you set out to make? Probably not. There are quite simply hundreds of stumbling blocks to be negotiated and difficult decisions to be made while brewing, and the chance that you have handled them all perfectly is rather unlikely. This is the reason that the same recipe made by two different people, or in two different places, will only very rarely turn out the same beer. If nothing else, beer is an incredibly temperamental concoction.

Yet, despite all of these variables and potential complications—and I haven't even begun to discuss equipment problems, the infection hazards or supply difficulties—we still demand great taste and absolute consistency from our commercial brewers. And it is to the eternal credit of the men and women who command this continent's breweries that they actually meet these demands more often than not, and do so in a vast variety of styles.

SPEAKING OF STYLE

Anyone who is in the least bit familiar with the brewing of beer, whether at home, in a brew-on-premises shop or at a commercial operation, knows the importance of stylistic guidelines. These definitions of beer type are, after all, what guide a brewer to use specific ingredients and processes when he or she wishes to make a specific type of beer. For the brewer, these guidelines are invaluable.

For the nonbrewing beer drinker, on the other hand, stylistic guidelines hold much less importance and may even occasionally complicate matters rather than elucidate them. Does the casual consumer really need to know, for example, the technical brewing qualifications that govern a German-style pils? Probably not. For most beer drinkers, style is just something that they read on the label; they feel that their taste buds are enough to tell them whether a beer is good or bad. And they are probably right.

The truth is that style is fast becoming a questionable method of beer categorization in North America. To begin with, the lines separating various styles are increasingly being blurred and redefined. An Oregonian brown ale, for example, may possess the same degree of bitterness as an East Coast pale ale, and it is quite possible that any given triad of porter, dry stout and oatmeal stout, picked at random, will share a great number of flavor traits.

Then there are the (intentionally?) misleading labels that are slapped on beers by breweries large and small. Does Molson's Red Dog brand become an alt simply because the label says it is, even though the beer itself is a blend of lager and ale? Are we expected to accept without question the assertion that Miller's Reserve Velvet Stout is a true stout despite its unusually mild character? Are the ales brewed by Whistler Brewing really to be considered true ales irrespective of the fact that they are bottom-fermented? And what of the Cranberry Lambic released seasonally by the Boston Beer Company, a beer purported to be of a style that is confined by definition to a restricted area of Belgium? Such misleading labels are rife within the industry and only serve to further obfuscate the definitions of style.

Of course, when speaking of labels, it is impossible to ignore the new so-called "styles" that have flourished in North America under a variety of names. Take, for example, "amber beer"... please. There are so many "ambers" dotting the beerscape that it is virtually impossible to sort them out any longer. They can be lagers like Molson's Signature Series Amber Lager or ales like St. Stan's Amber Alt; mild in flavor as with the Amber of Wild Boar Brewing or intense like the Hart (Ontario) Amber Ale; and now, thanks to the Spring Street Brewing Company, they can even be spiced with cumin as with their Amber Wit.

Nowhere was this daffy definition dilemma better illustrated than at the 1993 Great American Beer Festival, held at the height of amber madness, where beers with "amber" in their names won medals in three different style classes, *not one of which was the Amber Ale category*! But even the 1993 GABF did not represent the absolute pinnacle of the brewing industry's color obsession. No, that was left to Labatt in early 1995 when the brewery launched a new beer, and a new style, simply named Copper.

STYLE — WHAT STYLE?

Just as the recognition of grape styles should be the starting point for anyone interested in wine, aficionados are well advised to get to know their styles if they wish to maximize their beer enjoyment. However, unlike the orderly grape-variety-to-wine-style relationship that exists in enology, beer styles are largely interpretive, and how you interpret them will have a great bearing on how you approach beer enjoyment.

If a wine maker wishes to make a chardonnay wine, he or she must start with a chardonnay grape, plain and simple. The option of using a pinot or a cabernet grape to yield a chardonnay wine simply does not exist, and the foolish wine maker who tries to get away with it will soon find that his or her winery will be out of business.

The brewer who wants to produce a pale ale, on the other hand, is able to start with the same basic ingredients as the brewer who desires a best bitter, IPA or brown ale. What will define the beer style will be dependent on how much of each ingredient is used, when they are added to the beer, the percentage of alpha acids contained in the hops, the hardness of the water and dozens of other variables. And even then, the absolute decision will likely be made not by the brewer but by the consumer.

There are relatively few beers in the world that are generally considered so stylistically perfect that they actually define their styles, and there are hundreds of others with stylistic integrity that is beyond reproach. There are many, many more, however, that reside on the fringes of stylistic definition and it is this group that prompts much discussion among home brewers and beer lovers.

I have seen many a glass of beer downed while a debate raged over whether Beer A merited inclusion in the pale ale category, as it claimed on the label, or whether it should be shoved into the brown ale class, instead. Once, I even came across a beer list in a brewpub that called into question the label classifications of the brands from an area microbrewery. Find a spirited beer-based discussion in your local beer bar or brewpub and the odds are that it will revolve around style.

Often forgotten during these spirited discussions is a very important — the most important — point: Does the beer taste good? After all, we do not drink beer to locate one that hits the stylistic requirements of its type perfectly; we drink beer to enjoy it. And if that enjoyment includes style analysis, well, that is just fine, but care should be taken not to get too hung up on whether a brew fits its label billing precisely. Far better to enjoy your glass of beer for what it is — and leave the labels to the designers and marketers.

The beauty of Labatt's Copper wasn't so much in the emergence of a new "color style" but in the fact that the brewery did not even know whether this new style was to be a lager or an ale! Thus, the marketing minds at the company decided to release two beers, one a lager and the other an ale, and have the public vote on which they preferred. The winner, proclaimed on Super Bowl Sunday, became Labatt Copper and presumably defined the "copper beer style" for all time. (For the record, the winner was the lager, a beer best described as a cross between the Canadian and Vienna lager styles.)

Yet despite this multitude of reasons that style is losing its meaning, there's still a lot to be said for maintaining a casual acquaintance with the variety of beer styles. It doesn't take a brewing chemist to realize that if people are going to match beer styles to foods or be able to select the appropriate beer for every occasion, they would do well to have at least cursory knowledge of what each different beer type is supposed to taste like. At the same time, though, they hardly need an in-depth awareness of the peculiarities of every style and spin-off interpretation. The solution, then, would appear to be to begin with the basics and work forward from there.

FAMILY TIES

The most fundamental, defining element of beer style, and the one most essential to beer understanding, is the separation between top- and bottom-fermentation. For it is in the fermenter that a beer's first "family" links are forged and there, too, that the most general aspects of a beer's flavor are defined.

Top-fermentation denotes beers that are fermented in warmer temperatures and, generally speaking, aged for shorter periods of time than their bottom-fermented brethren. These brews are commonly identified as being of the ale class, even though stouts and wheats and other styles are also top-fermented, and the reason they are known as top-fermenting beers is that they employ yeast strains that work up to the top of the fermenting vessel. As a general rule, and of particular importance to the beer taster, these beers will tend toward characters that are fruity and quite possibly sweet, even though those qualities may be obscured by bitter hopping as is the case with many of the ales of the Pacific Northwest.

Over beer's 5,000-year history, top-fermentation has been the rule for at least four-fifths of the time. I say "at least" because no one is completely sure exactly when bottom-fermentation came into the picture, but it is a fair guess that it was being practiced, albeit unknowingly, around the time of the Norman Invasion, in 1066, in what is now Germany. In the years since, especially over the last century, bottom-fermentation has come to dominate its older brother in the global market, making lager the most popular beer style the world over. Generally speaking, and I emphasize that this is a generalization of the highest order, bottom-fermented beers will emerge with crisper, drier characters.

Up until very recently, these fermentation separations were essential in defining beer styles. If a beer was labeled an ale, you could be reasonably sure that it had been top-fermented and, conversely, if a second beer was identified as a lager, you could rest assured that it had been bottom-fermented. This is no longer the case. Advances in brewing technology and yeast handling have given birth to ales fermented by lager yeasts (as with the Whistler ales) and top-fermented lagers (such as the lager of Wellington County) and, although the site of fermentation is still of importance to the characters of most beers, it is no longer the absolute, dominant factor that it once was. In today's brewing reality, it is quite possible to produce a completely credible ale using a bottom-fermenting yeast and vice versa, although I would argue that greatness still lies only at the traditional end of the fermenting tank.

But, on this continent at least, fermentation site is not the most common way of separating beer into families. For image-obsessed North Americans, the only way to categorize beer is by hue.

Anyone even remotely interested in the beer industry has, by now, certainly digested their fill of arbitrary color distinctions and claims. The 1990s have seen an unprecedented interest in beer shades, from the Coors television ad campaign (for their Extra Gold brand) that asked passersby to evaluate two beers on the basis of their colors, to the Labatt rhetoric (for *both* Coppers) about combining the "full flavor... of a dark beer" with the "refreshing" nature of a mainstream — that is, light-colored — beer. With such misleading color-consciousness flooding the media, it is no wonder that beer drinkers commonly make flavor assessments based purely on the shade of a beer.

In reality, though, color has only a loose connection to taste. A darker beer may indeed have a full body and dynamic flavor, or it may simply have a little roasted malt added to the mash for aesthetic effect. Similarly, a pale-hued brew may taste as light as it looks, or it may have a huge bitter or fruity character. As the old saying goes, you can't judge a book by its cover. Or a beer by its color.

To check out color-flavor relationships for yourself, simply try the following test. While blindfolded, have a friend give you samples of four or five different ales, or the same number of different lagers, making sure that some of them are light in color and others dark. Taste each one and try to distinguish the light beers from the darker ones; chances are, you will be very surprised when you remove your blindfold at the end of the test.

Despite the misleading nature of color, however, it is useful in some beer-tasting instances. A stout, for example, should never stray any lighter than dark brown and a pilsner should not emerge from the aging tank any darker than a medium gold. What's more, brewers go to a lot of trouble to obtain specific colors for their brews, with occasionally beautiful results, and it would be a massive oversight on the taster's part to not appreciate this aspect of a beer. The visual is, after all, an aesthetic consideration that plays a pivotal role in human enjoyment of all forms. An aficionado's best bet is to observe and savor a beer's color, but not be guided by it.

The third and final basic beer classification concerns whether or not a beer is particularly hoppy. The intense hopping of a beer will yield a wide spectrum of flavors depending on the style of beer as well as the type of hops used, but the single most defining characteristic will be bitterness in the body. Lightly hopped brews, on the other hand, will display more of the grain character in the form of flavors varying from cereal in light lagers to fruits, coffee and anise in ales and stouts. As major brewery products tend to be so lightly hopped as to be almost unnoticeable, this categorization is most useful when describing craft-brewed beers.

In addition to adding bitterness to the brew, hops are also responsible for the main part of a beer's aroma. In this regard, the scents can range tremendously, from fresh-cut flowers to nuts to dried leaf to grapefruit and citrus, and because of this variety, it is unwise to make generalizations about hop aroma. Each separate hop genus will add its own distinctive notes to the nose, and the sum total of the hops, malt and the effects of the yeast will yield a final aroma individually suited to that particular beer.

As a general rule, beer drinkers who have little or no experience with craft-brewed beers will recoil from the aroma and taste of well-hopped brews. This reaction occurs for no other reason than their unfamiliarity with the style, since the big-brewery beers they have been drinking are unlikely to have had much in hop character. A little time and tasting, though, will adapt even the most hop-fearful among us to a diversity of marvelous hoppy brews, from pale ales to German-style pils.

BEER STYLES OF NORTH AMERICA

Having defined the basics, it is now time to turn to the specifics of beer style as they apply to the North American beerscape. This is not a task without pitfalls aplenty.

The difficulty in trying to catalogue this continent's beer styles is deciding where to stop. Does one, for example, list steinbiers — brews heated by

REINHEITSGE-WHAT?

The rise of the craft brewing industry has brought many a new word or phrase into the North American lexicon. Terms like "microbrewing," "brewpub," "all-malt" and even "cold-filtered" have all become part of our language due to the influence of this new field of brewing, either directly or indirectly. No new expression, however, has caused as much confusion or misinterpretation as that awkward (for anglophones) word North American brewers have borrowed from their German counterparts: Reinheitsgebot.

Also known as the Bavarian Purity Law of 1516, the Reinheitsgebot (Rine-heights-ge-bote) is the German act that limits the ingredients allowed in brewing to water, yeast, hops and barley, plus wheat for weizens. Despite the fact that the European Union has rendered such a law unenforceable, the vast majority of German brewers have elected to stick by the act in the belief that adherence is the only way to assure the quality of their beer, and for the same reason, many North American microbrewers have adopted it, as well. But does the Reinheitsgebot mean good beer?

The answer is yes, and no. Like most issues in the brewing world, there is considerable controversy over whether the maintenance of Reinheitsgebot standards is instrumental to the brewing of good beer. Some trumpet it as the only standard by which the quality of one's brewing may be judged while others feel that it is unnecessarily limiting. I believe both sides are right.

When bottom-fermenting beer, purity and cleanliness and an unadulterated supply of ingredients are of paramount importance to the quality of your finished beer. As such, the stricter the control of the ingredients and the conditions under which they are employed, the better the final lager will be. Moreover, insofar as lagers tend to be crisper and cleaner in taste, the use of extra or substitute ingredients will show more directly in the flavor of the beer. For lager brewing, then, the Reinheitsgebot makes all sorts of sense.

Shift your focus to the top of the fermenting tank, however, and the Reinheitsgebot gets thrown right out the window. Witness, for example, the many spices and brewing sugars used in Belgian brewing methods or the normal use of corn grits in British-style ale brewing. These techniques result in some of the best beers in the world, none of which are Reinheitsgebot-pure. With all the fruity esters and various other flavors that are common in top-fermented beer, there is simply more leeway than that allowed in lager brewing.

So, yes, seeing that the brewery proudly endorses the Reinheitsgebot on their label does guarantee you purity in your beer, but it does not say anything about how good it will taste.

the addition of incredibly hot stones — because a lone American brewery happens to produce one? Do rye beers merit inclusion because they are brewed from time to time by several different breweries? And how about the new crop of blended beers, such as black and tans, where the "style" is actually two styles mixed together at the bottling line?

Nor do the difficulties stop at the fringe beer styles; several common types of beer can be similarly problematic when placed in a North American context. American pale ale has quite rightfully been added to the list of international beer styles, but practically every style of beer in the world can be said to have a North American interpretation, so where does one stop? And even when that line in the grain has been drawn, what of the regional interpretations that make an Oregonian hefe-weizen differ from the Quebec version and cause a gulf of stylistic differences to grow between ales from California and those from New York?

In an attempt to sort through all of the above questions and quandaries, I have limited the following catalogue of style to the most common types of beer brewed in North America today. This means that you will not find such country-specific styles as lambic (Belgium) or Berliner weisse (Germany), nor are such obscure varieties as the above-mentioned steinbier listed. Regardless of where you live, you should not have trouble finding an example of most of the styles catalogued below.

As a short preamble to this similarly abbreviated North American beer dictionary, I must emphasize that the following are consumer definitions only and that anyone wishing more detail on beer varieties is advised to investigate any or all of the excellent style guides listed in Appendix II. Also, because words can only accomplish so much, I have listed examples of each style following its definition. These may or may not be widely available beers, but they do represent the styles well. Try them, and see for yourself!

A Concise Catalogue
of North American Beer Styles

TOP-FERMENTED

Amber Ale

Although amber ale is perhaps most accurately typified as a style without a definition, a few common threads may be joined together to form a crude picture of this most North American of beer types. Bear in mind, though, that amber ale is without question the most widely and the most loosely interpreted style on this continent.

While one can be forgiven for thinking that an amber ale should be amber, most often they range from medium gold to deep rust in color. Aromas will vary widely, but should be defined more by the malt than by the hopping—although even pale ales sometimes masquerade as ambers.

The body of an amber ale is likewise open to interpretation, but should also be influenced greatly by the malt. As amber is the North American version of the "session ale"—that is, easy-drinking—it should also be a beer that will not weigh too heavily on the palate or stomach.

Examples: Algonquin Special Reserve Ale, Great Divide Arapahoe Amber Ale.

Belgian-Style Ale (Abbey Ale, Tripel)

To categorize Belgian-style ales under one heading is to attempt the impossible. So in deference to that country's wide variety of quirky top-fermented styles, I am limiting this section to the two styles most commonly brewed in North America.

The abbey ale and tripel are, at the same time, similar and quite different. The abbey should be earthy brown while the tripel tends toward light to medium gold, and the abbey's complex, spicy aroma contrasts with the tripel's medium-dry, sometimes fruity, nose. That said, however, tripels are often characterized as stronger, blond versions of abbey ales.

In the body, too, there are similarities and dramatic differences. The abbey will be earthier with notes of chocolate or spice, but will also show some of the zest and fruitiness possessed by the tripel. The tripel, on the other hand, will have a cleaner, crisper character. Another difference—

the abbey should be served at cellar temperature whereas the tripel can be served at cellar or refrigerator temperature. Both styles will be bottle-fermented.

Examples: New Belgium Abbey Trappist Style Ale, Unibroue La Fin du Monde (tripel).

Bitter (Best Bitter, Extra Special Bitter)

"A pint of your best" is a phrase oft-spoken over the years by many a British pub-goer, and it was not meant in reference to the pub's finest beer. The object of the customer's desire would be a best bitter, and while you would still be unlikely to get the same reaction to such a request in a Chicago bar, these fine ales have become quite popular among North American microbrewers.

Although some will still insist that a bitter is just the draft version of the house pale ale, these amber- to rust-colored brews have come to represent a style all their own over the years. The aroma of a bitter will tend toward a leafiness, particularly if it has been dry-hopped, but some maltiness should be in evidence, as well.

The body of a bitter should come close to that of a pale ale, but possess more of a malty character, particularly relative to the American pale. It should also be softer and less assertive, and while it may not show in the taste, it will also likely possess a lower alcohol content, likely in the 3.5%–5% by volume range.

Examples: Conners Best Bitter, Wynkoop ESB.

Brown Ale

Having originated in the blue-collar regions of northeast England, it comes as no surprise that brown ale is a style designed for easy drinking at the end of a hardworking day. Alternately satisfying and refreshing, normally without a terribly high alcohol content (4–5% by volume), brown ale is the perfect style to select when setting up for a long night at the pub.

True to its moniker, brown ale should be brown in color, while the aroma should not speak overly of hops. A balanced blend of nutty and fruity notes will generally signify a worthy brown ale, with some woodiness occasionally showing in American browns.

Like the aroma, the body should not be too hoppy, but a certain degree of dryness is essential to the style. Expect some fruity or caramel malt notes along with an assertive nuttiness and, above all, an easy drinkability.

Examples: Hart Festive Brown Ale, Oregon Nut Brown Ale.

Canadian Ale

One of the many ale and ale-hybrid styles that developed during the commercial onslaught of lagers in the early 1900s, Canadian ale has been reinvented several times over through the years and is now normally but a faint imitation of the traditional style. This is a pity, because it can be a very enjoyable beer when brewed as it was originally meant to be.

As might be expected of a style that arose in response to the lager invasion, a Canadian ale should be golden in color with balanced malt and hops showing in the aroma. Notes to look for in the nose include fruit, light spice and grain.

The body of a Canadian ale should have a fullness and, perhaps, a fruitiness that speaks of the top-fermenting yeast. A slightly creamy character would not be out of place, nor would a moderate degree of complex hoppiness or notes of spice.

Examples: O'Keefe Ale (modern style), Catamount Gold (traditional style).

German-Style Ales (Alt, Kölsch)

While southern German brewers have long been justifiably lauded for their bottom-fermented gems, the top-fermented and cold-conditioned beers of their more northern counterparts have been largely ignored through the years. Thankfully, this has now changed and altbier and kölsch are recognized as regional treasures, so much so, in fact, that they are growing in popularity among American brewers.

Though related by their country of origin and basic methods, alt and kölsch differ quite markedly. Kölsch will be golden in color, contrasting with the copper-brown of an alt, and the former will have a fresh, lightly fruity aroma while the latter will possess a hoppier nose with more earthiness.

In the body, the two styles contrast yet again. Kölsch will tend to be almost delicate in its maltiness with a light, acidic hopping drying it out to its refreshing, faintly herbal character. An alt, on the other hand, will be more assertively hopped and therefore bitter, with a much fainter fruitiness. Both styles are brewed sporadically, and with varying degrees of success, in North America.

Examples: St. Stan's Amber Alt, Goose Island Kölsch.

Pale Ale *(American Pale Ale, British Pale Ale, India Pale Ale)*

Pale ale is a style that perhaps has more regional interpretations than any other, save pilsner and wheat. It originated as a paler, more highly hopped ale in Britain, brewed in response to the porters and dark ales that were popular some 200 to 300 years ago. It has since gone on to develop many local variations, the most recent being the American one.

Anyone expecting a pale ale to be pale in color will be seriously disappointed; its name is derived from its lighter hue relative only to porters, stouts and dark ales, although India pale ales (IPAs) will be more coppery in color. In any of its incarnations, it should have a hoppy and complex aroma, ranging from the fruit and wood notes common to the English style to the more floral character of an American pale or the intense, grapefruity bitter-sourness of some IPAs.

Hops should also take a major role in the body of a pale ale, again regardless of type. English pales tend to have their hoppiness held in check by a degree of maltiness that may show as fruit, while American pales will demonstrate a much more pronounced, woody and bitter hoppiness. India pale ales, which derive their name from the high rates of hopping used to preserve ales during the long sea journey from Europe to India, will have rates of hopping that may be so high they will put off all but the hardiest of hop lovers.

Examples: Catamount Christmas Ale (IPA), Pike Place Pale Ale (British), Sierra Nevada Pale Ale (American).

Porter

Porters preceded stouts in brewing history and are reputedly so named because they were the preferred drink of the porters of English seaside towns. In a brewery making both a porter and a stout, the porter will be the milder of the two but should be in the same ballpark in terms of taste. The exception to this rule is the strong, sweet and usually bottom-fermented porter style common to areas of eastern Europe.

Ranging from dark brown to nearly black in color, a porter should have various levels of roastiness in the aroma as well as a fair dose of coffee, chocolate, anise or soft fruit, or a combination of the four. Strong porters will have less intense and decidedly fruitier aroma notes.

The fruitier notes of strong porters should also show in the body and some of these beers even begin to resemble port wines. In the top-fermented style, the roast of the aroma should likewise show in the body along with a varied combination of the other aroma notes. If a porter becomes too strong in its flavor, it really should be renamed a stout.

Examples: Redhook Blackhook Porter, Okanagan Olde English Porter (strong).

Scottish Ale / Scotch Ale

The beers of Scotland run the gamut from light to very heavy in terms of alcohol content, with the stronger type generally known as Scotch, rather than Scottish, ales. The constant in all of them, however, is that they are full-bodied ales with a particular knack for warding off the chill of a rainy fall night.

Because they are styled as very malty beers, Scottish ales will tend to be dark brown to almost black (for Scotch ales) in color and strongly malty in their aroma. Although their aromas may have a small amount of fruitiness to them, the malt is more likely to show in caramel or toffee notes, and the hop should be barely discernible.

The bodies of all Scottish and Scotch ales will be sweet, with the level of sweetness increasing relative to the alcohol level. They should also have malty complexity to their tastes and possess particularly satisfying characters. A Scotch ale should be very full-bodied and warmingly alcoholic.

Examples: Portland Brewing McTarnahan's Ale, Vermont Pub and Brewery Wee Heavy (Scotch).

Stout (Dry Stout, Sweet Stout, Oatmeal Stout, Imperial Stout)

Originally known as "stout porter" and thus often referred to as porter's big brother, stout is an enigmatic style that takes several forms. That people are often scared away from these ebony marvels by the depth of their color is perhaps the saddest consequence of any misconception in brewing.

Regardless of its substyle, stout should be deep brown to jet black in color. Dry, oatmeal and imperial stouts will have varying levels of forceful, roasty aromas, while the sweet, strong and often bottom-fermented stouts particularly popular in the Caribbean may get quite plummy or develop raw sugar notes. (Note that the sweet stouts discussed here differ from the sweet stouts, often called milk stouts, still brewed sporadically in the United Kingdom.)

Of all the substyles that exist of various types of beer, perhaps none are as dissimilar as those of stout. Dry stouts will tend toward burnt, coffee-ish bodies; sweet stouts will very much resemble strong porters and have much-reduced levels of roastiness and a sugary, fruity or faintly lactic quality; oatmeals will be silky and smooth with varying levels of porridge in their bodies; and imperial stouts will be forceful, alcoholic and even winy. In any form, a stout should be a fortifying tipple.

Examples: Desnoes and Geddes Dragon Stout (sweet), Sierra Nevada Stout (dry), St. Ambroise Oatmeal Stout, Wellington County Imperial Stout.

Strong Ale / Barley Wine

For beer drinkers accustomed to major-label beers that top out at 5–6% alcohol by volume, it comes as quite a shock to find that some strong ales and barley wines reach the dizzying heights of 8–10% and as much as 14%! But reach it they do and, when properly executed, they do it with style, finesse and surprising subtlety.

There is great range among strong ales and barley wines, but most will fall into the color scope of rust to dark brown and carry forceful aromas containing a variety of fruits. Varying degrees of hoppiness and alcoholic notes that may resemble port wine or even whisky will play a role in their bouquets.

There will be at least moderate sweetness apparent in any strong ale, even if it may become buried under the weight of heavy hopping, and alcohol should always be in evidence in some fashion. The most important aspect of any example of these two styles, however, is that it should not bully the consumer. After all, these are not shots of rotgut whisky meant to be thrown back in haste, but silken pleasures created for hours of enjoyment.

Examples: Niagara Falls Olde Jack Strong Ale, Sierra Nevada, Bigfoot Barley Wine.

Other International Variations

British mild ale, sparkling ale, Irish ale, Belgian red ale and other ales particular to that country, steinbier, British sweet stout (also known as milk stout).

BOTTOM-FERMENTED

Bock *(Doppelbock, Pale Bock, Eisbock)*

When I was growing up in Quebec, the mythology surrounding bock beers stated that they were made from the residue gathered from the brewing kettle during its spring cleaning. This couldn't be further from the truth; bocks are the strong brews of Germany and can be glorious brewing creations.

At one time, all bocks were dark. While this is still true of most, several breweries do brew paler versions instead of, or in addition to, bocks of the traditional amber-rust to deep purple tones. The aroma of a bock should be sweet and full, extremely so in the case of the stronger doppelbock. Complexity of sweetness is, of course, desired, but overly fruity or sugary notes are to be avoided.

Like their aromas, bocks should taste sweet without being sugary or dominantly fruity. The body of a bock must have complexity and style, otherwise it is just a strong lager. Look for chocolate or mocha notes, and perhaps some spiciness or woody hop. In the doppelbock, the flavors should be more intense and portlike notes of alcohol may show, as well. Eisbock, a version made by concentrating the beer through freezing, will have flavors as intense as a doppelbock, but in a drier character.

Examples: Brasal Bock, Samuel Adams Double Bock, Sierra Nevada Pale Bock, Niagara Falls Eisbock.

Dunkel

After the discovery of bottom-fermentation and cold lagering (storage) but before the invention of pilsner, there were dark lagers. Today, in deference to their Germanic origins, these beers are sometimes referred to as dunkels. In North America, however, they are most often simply called dark lagers and in some cases, may simply be a darker version of a brewery's regular lager.

Not surprisingly, a dunkel should be dark in color, somewhere in the neighborhood of medium to dark brown. Their aromas should be malt-dominated with some balancing floral hopping. Look for light chocolate or toffee notes and a degree of burnt wood.

The body of a dunkel will likewise be malt-dominated, with a mildly sweet and perhaps slightly spicy character. It should not, however, be cloying or overly sweet, nor too dry, nutty or roasty. There may be a touch of acidity toward the finish that will dry out the taste.

Examples: Frankenmuth Dark, Vancouver Island Hermann's Dark Lager.

Malt Liquor

More of a strength indicator than a style *per se*, malt liquors are strong lagers usually designed without great concern for subtlety. Because they are classed by strength, however, a few gems occasionally get stuck in the category, as well.

Normally light to medium gold in color, malt liquors will sometimes show a little color in their cheeks. The aromas of these strong brews tend to be malty, although without complexity in most cases. Exceptions to the complexity rule will demonstrate a slight roastiness and a round sweetness.

Malt liquors are not made to be coy. They are upfront in their tastes with notable alcohol and an enhanced American or Canadian lager character. The exceptions to these general malt liquor rules of thumb may demonstrate brandy-like strength, flavorful complexity and mild to moderate hopping.

Examples: Schlitz Red Bull, Upper Canada Rebellion (premium style).

North American Lager *(American Lager, Canadian Lager, Ice Beer, Light)*

Taken together, these four almost indiscernible styles probably account for some 98 percent of all the beer consumed in North America. This would be a sad state of affairs regardless of which style was dominant because there is so much more to the world of beer, but it is made even worse by the fact that these are the most mundane styles listed in these pages.

All of these styles should range from light yellow to light gold in color and have sweet, grainy aromas. Anything more than very light hop notes will likely only be present in the nose of a Canadian lager, and even then they will not be overly significant.

These styles are designed to appeal to the widest audience possible and so they will not possess any overpowering flavor notes. The general character of each will be sweet and grainy, with a slightly bigger malt character evident in the Canadian lager and a cleaner taste showing in the ice.

Note that while in the United States, "light" signifies a beer with fewer calories, in Canada the term identifies a lower-strength beer.

Examples: Budweiser, Labatt Blue, Molson Ice, Miller Lite.

Pilsner / Pils *(Bohemian, Continental, German)*

While bottom-fermentation has been in use for an indeterminate length of time, pilsner brewing was first developed in 1842 in Pilsen, Czech Republic, the town after which the style is named. It was a development that would eventually reshape the way the world viewed beer.

A light gold color will characterize all three pilsners, while the aromas will differ slightly. The Bohemian style will normally possess a floral, hoppy aroma whereas the German type will have a more assertive and leafy or woody hopping and the continental type will be essentially a scaled-down version of the German pilsner.

In the body, all three will have varying levels of dryness, with the Bohemian leading the way, followed very closely by the German and then the continental. Hopping will dominate the taste of all three, with continental again having the least assertive personality, but the Bohemian pilsner may tend toward a softer, more floral character than the aggressive German.

Examples: Brasal Hopps Bräu (German), Stoudt Pilsener (Bohemian), August Schell Pils (Continental).

Vienna Lager *(Märzen, Festbier)*

Although adorned with the name of an Austrian city, today's Vienna lager is actually an amalgamation of a style developed by a brewery in that city and an evolution of that style that took place in and around Munich, Germany. The latter city also developed the märzen or festbier style as an offshoot, so named because the German brewers would brew extra beer in March (Märzen), before the warm weather made prerefrigeration brewing impossible, and store it in cold caves for the fall festivals.

The color of a Vienna should be amber-red, but a märzen can range from medium gold to light brown. The aroma in both cases should present the malt up front, with toasty and spicy notes, and balance and dry it out with light hopping. Märzens should have a more pronounced malt character than Viennas.

The body of a Vienna should be smooth, graceful, sweet and spicy.

The märzen should likewise emulate these characteristics, but a little light fruitiness is also allowable in this slightly (about 1–1.5%) stronger and maltier cousin. In the Vienna, there may also be a subtle, drying hop present, particularly toward the finish, but it should not be at all invasive to the taste.

Examples: Thomas Kemper Integrale (Vienna), Heckler Bräu Fest Märzen.

Other International Variations

Dortmunder Export (also known simply as export), Munich Helles, American Amber Lager.

WHEAT BEERS

Although they are top-fermented like ales, wheat beers really do belong in a separate and distinct class all their own. They are quirky, decidedly individualistic and, some say, combine the best elements of an ale with the refreshing character of a lager.

The amount of wheat present in a wheat beer can range from as little as 10–20 percent to as much as 60 percent of the mash and it may be used in malted or unmalted forms, or a combination of the two. The wheat grain itself serves to lighten the body of the finished beer and provide it with a refreshingly sour character. This effect is why wheats are often chosen as the bases upon which fruit or spiced beers are built. A beer that has wheat in it, however, is not necessarily a wheat beer; numerous ales will use small amounts of wheat for head retention and other factors, as well.

When exploring the world of wheats, it is important to understand that, at least among North American wheats, what you see may not necessarily be what you get. It could very well be that the beer you buy labeled "weisse" might turn out to be a wheat ale, or you may find that the new microbrewed "wheat beer" you find could be a wit in disguise. When it comes to wheats, it seems, a lot of breweries are still unsure of how to best match up the style with the name tag.

American Wheat Ale

Many breweries, particularly those that brew ales exclusively, use this style as their "starter" beer, designed to attract major brewery consumers to craft-brewed fare. In this role, its lightness and lack of bold character serve the American wheat well.

The American wheat ale will be light in color, usually yellow to medium gold, and will normally have a particularly grainy aroma. Depending on the amount of wheat used and the hops present, the aroma may also show notes of citrus or a small amount of spiciness.

The body of an American wheat will be not unlike that of a light ale, except without much of the fruity sweetness and definitely without a big hop character. The wheat may contribute a lemony taste, but the overall flavor will be dry, grainy and perhaps a bit sour.

Examples: Anchor Wheat Beer, Big Rock Grasshopper Wheat Ale.

Weisse / Weizen

This pair of designations denotes wheat beer of a style originally found in southern Germany. Until the rise of the American Wheat ale style in the early 1990s, this was also the most common form of wheat beer brewed in North America.

A weisse should be light to medium gold in color, unless it is specifically designated as dunkel, meaning dark. It may or may not appear cloudy from the addition of a dosage of yeast to the bottle and it should be very spritzy and active when poured. (Weizens affixed with the prefix *hefe* — hefe-weizen — should always have been dosed with yeast.)

The aroma should normally be characterized by notes of spice, particularly clove, and/or bubblegummy or banana-like notes. Sometimes citrus, particularly lemon, will also creep into the mix, but that has nothing to do with the slice of lemon you will often find on the side of your glass when you order your weisse in a bar or restaurant.

The body of a weisse will range from full to medium in character but should always be refreshing and free of significant hop influence. Flavors to look for are banana, clove and lemon, although neither of the first two are likely to be present unless the brewery is using a true German wheat yeast, and the finish should not be too cloying. A dunkel weizen will approximate the same character, but with a light roastiness or chocolate character to it.

Examples: Lakefront Weisse, Widmer Hefe-Weizen, Samuel Adams Dunkel Weizen.

Wit / White

The rarest of wheat styles in North America, white beer is Belgian in origin and was brought to this continent by the same man who resurrected it from the pages of the history books in Belgium, Pierre Celis. It is arguably the most refreshing of the three wheat styles presented here.

By definition, wit must have yeast in the bottle and should be served with this yeast suspended in the beer. This action gives it its shimmering, sandy color and when the light hits it just right, demonstrates why it is known as white beer.

Insofar as wits are normally brewed with coriander, orange peel and a mixture of other spices, it comes as no surprise that these elements will dominate both the aroma and flavor. There should also be a level of tanginess in the body, a result of the wheat used in this style being unmalted, and the overall character should be crisp and invigorating.

Examples: Unibroue Blanche de Chambly, Celis White.

Other International Variations

Belgian lambic and gueuze (site-specific), Berliner weisse (site-specific), wheat bock, flavored wheat beers.

SPECIALTIES AND ODDITIES

With the arrival to North American shores of spiced and fruit beers and strong, intense ales and bocks, the doors were thrown wide open to just about every imaginable interpretation of beer. Pumpkin ales, cumin-spiced wheats, garlic beers, brews flavored with chocolate, maple or chilies; the only limits left on how beer could taste seemed to be the imagination of the brewer and the degree to which the consumer was willing to experiment.

While some stuck-in-the-mud traditionalists feel that these new brews are but bastardizations of legitimate styles, my view is that, at their best, they offer marvelous new taste experiences and even at their worst, they are still helpful in expanding the limits of beer appreciation. This does not mean that I want to drink these brews all the time, just that I am happy they are there.

Due to this newfound beery freedom of expression, a complete listing of specialty beer types in North America could go on *ad infinitum*, with virtually every fruit or spice in circulation meriting mention. Rather than attempt such a monumental feat, the following catalogue of specialties lists only the most basic of style definitions, as well as a couple of uniquely North American styles that are particularly deserving of mention.

Christmas / Festival Beer

Truly a specialty without limits, festival beers are born from a brewery's desire to celebrate a particular season or event. Often these brews end up being quite spectacular because, being seasonals or one-offs, the brewery will frequently become more experimental in their production.

The only constant in the festival beer style is that it should be a fairly unusual beer for that brewery. This unique character could take many forms, from doppelbock to strong ale to fruit beer to spiced beer. The important thing is that the consumer should find it to be special.

Common festival beer types include strong ales or bocks (Portland Brewing Icicle Creek Ale, Vancouver Island Hermannator), heavily hopped ales (Rogue Mogul) and spiced beers (Our Special Ale from Anchor).

Cream Ale

An original North American style, cream ale combines a warm, ale-type fermentation (using either ale or lager yeast) with a cold, lager-style conditioning. It was developed in the early twentieth century by ale breweries wishing to compete in the increasingly popular lager market.

Light to medium gold in color, a cream ale should appear to the eye much like a lager, with good carbonation and an active head. It should also be relatively well hopped in the aroma with some, but not too much, fruit showing, as well.

The body of a cream ale should be fairly light and refreshing, again much like a lager. Due to the warm ferment, however, some ale-like fruitiness or round, malty character is also desirable. Occasionally, a cream ale will be a blend of a given brewery's lager and ale, although this practice is becoming increasingly rare.

Examples: Little Kings Cream Ale, Sleeman Cream Ale.

FLAVORED BEERS

As noted in the preamble to this section, virtually any fruit, spice or flavoring is allowable in a beer these days, providing that the consumer will drink it! Beyond that very important qualification, anything goes.

Traditionally, the fruit beers of Belgium have used two berries; cherries (for kriek) and raspberries (for framboise). In North America, however, you can add pumpkin, blueberry and cranberry to these two in the ever-evolving and growing list of preferred fruits. And in the spice category, the doors have been thrown open ever wider, with everything from coriander to chili peppers being awarded a place in the brewing kettle.

The important quality any flavored beer must possess is balance. The seasoning must never dominate the taste to the point of submission, but neither should it be present in name only. For this reason, the creation of a beer made with fruit, spices or other flavoring agents is among the most difficult challenges a brewer can face.

Examples: Hart Pyramid Apricot Ale, New Glarus Belgian Red.

Rauchbier / Smoked Beer

A specialty of German origin, rauchbier is simply beer brewed with barley malt that has been smoked prior to being used for brewing. In its original incarnation, it is normally a bottom-fermented beer, but North American breweries have been known to make smoked ales and porters, as well.

A proper smoked beer is not for the timid. It should be bold and upfront in its smokiness, even going so far as to evoke the image of an Islay whisky or a German smoked sausage. At the same time, however, the smoke should not push the flavor of the beer entirely to the sidelines. As with the flavored beers, balance is everything.

Examples: Alaskan Smoker Porter, Rogue Smoke.

Rousse

A top-fermented style that will be unfamiliar to even experienced beer connoisseurs, rousse was developed within the last decade in Quebec at a brewery called Les Brasseurs du Nord. After a short time, Molson followed up the rousse of Les Brasseurs with one of their own, and thus legitimized a budding and very individualistic beer style.

Rousse literally translates from the French to russet, and that is the color it should be. The aroma should be fruitier than a brown or Scottish ale, with perhaps a few notes of spice to it.

The body of a rousse ought to fall somewhere in the stylistic vacuum between brown ale, Scottish ale and Belgian abbey ale. It should have a strong fruitiness that begins softly and ends in a flourish of floral or leafy hopping. Borrowing from the Belgians, a rousse should also have a touch of quirkiness to its character.

Examples: Boréale Rousse.

Steam Beer

Also known as California common beer because of the Anchor Brewing Company's trademark on the name "steam beer," this is a hybrid style that developed in the early 1900s. It basically involves ale brewing with a lager yeast, but what makes it unique are the large, wading-pool-like vessels used for fermentation.

The color of a steam beer is medium gold to copper and the aroma should carry a combination of the complex fullness of an ale and the crisp hoppiness of a lager. Also look for notes of spice and faint fruit.

The body of a perfect steam beer should be dazzlingly complex. This is because it must marry a pilsner's refreshingly dry hoppiness with the full maltiness of a brown ale, and with lager-type carbonation, to boot! The resulting beer should hold some fruitiness as well as some dry woodiness, with the latter in particular evidence at the finish.

Examples: Anchor Steam Beer.

Other International Variations

Triple Bock (fermented with ale and champagne yeasts), Rye Beer, Black Beer (Schwarzbier), Honey Beer.

CHAPTER 3

ENJOYING LIFE...
WITH BEER

There is little doubt that beer is a hugely popular beverage in North America and even less question of its elevated status within the social fabric of the continent. Ironically, however, the style of beer that maintains this prestigious position among the hoi polloi is the least democratic of all brews. Love it or hate it, the North American lager is the supreme potentate of this continent's beer empire.

This is an unfortunate state of affairs because beer's position as the most democratic of drinks is well deserved. To begin with, even relatively expensive beer is by and large more affordable than wine, spirits, sherries, ports, liqueurs or any other alcoholic beverage, thus making it by far the most accessible of these beverages. Moreover, there are enough types and styles of beer to suit any occasion or disposition. But still, the dictatorial lager rules all, and, at the time of writing, accounts for a huge percentage of the total beer market.

It is not a benign dictator, either, this big-brewery, commercial-grade Canadian or American lager. It has scratched and clawed its way to the top and it will do anything, even spend millions upon millions of dollars, to maintain its position. Upstarts are simply not tolerated within its domain.

Because beer is so democratic, and my political-science past so enduring, I often muse on how beer styles reflect political thought, particularly in North America. Like the political spectrum, there are extremes in beer styles that range from the sublime to the ridiculous. Likewise, as with politics, there are varieties of expression within each and every style, from bold and unrelenting to mild and muted. Yet the dominant style, like the dominant field of political thought, occupies but a blip on the full range of possibilities.

North America's history is as filled with excursions into odd and assorted beer styles as it is with experiments in political thought. And just as fringe parties seem to regularly pop up in politics, fringe beer styles also enjoy sporadic exposure to the spotlight. Their methods of self-promotion are even similar: microbreweries are promoted through regional beer tabloids called "brewspapers" and small market magazines just as fringe parties have traditionally relied upon circulars and newsprint manifestos.

If there is a difference between beer styles and politics, it is that beer is even more democratic than politics: in political thought, there are but a finite number of positions on the spectrum and a fairly set count of interpretations within each point; with beer, however, there are many more styles than there are political ideologies and infinite numbers of interpretations within each view. So while an ale may base itself on the Sierra Nevada Pale Ale in the same way that a political party might base itself on Truman's or Trudeau's vision of their respective nations, the chances are far greater that the party, rather than the pale ale, will be more doctrinaire. There are, quite simply, many more beers than there are political parties.

Getting back to that dominant style, though, it is plain to see that politics and beer are diverging dramatically as the 1990s continue into the next century. Where political thought remains more or less as it has been for many years or even decades, beer thought is changing in a most revolutionary way. Beer lovers of every stripe are discovering the full spectrum of beer choices and reveling in their findings. This has given rise to a common concern, namely: How do I get into this microbeer thing?

GETTING TO KNOW YOU...

There are many ways to get to better know this food we call beer and, seeing as most people—most North Americans, at least—tend to think of beer as a single-utility beverage, the more ways there are to familiarize yourself with beer, the better!

Before becoming better acquainted with beer, however, it is first necessary to modify a few traditional North American attitudes toward this fine beverage.

CHANGING VIEWPOINTS

Unlike wine or whisky or vintage port, getting to know beer will not cost you an arm and a leg. However, it will probably cost more than you think.

Because of beer's inglorious recent past in North America, we have grown accustomed to paying a set price of no more than a dollar per bottle, and usually expect to pay considerably less. The very sound reasoning behind this price consciousness was based on the premise that all beers tasted more or less the same, which they did, so it became very hard to rationalize paying more than a few bucks for a six-pack of any particular beer.

Over the past decade or so, it has become very apparent that all beers do not taste the same, and thus, a pricing structure has been born. True, your mass-market lagers will still cost you that same few bucks per six, but other beers on the market may now run you two or three dollars per bottle, and in rare instances, even as much as five dollars or more! For many beer drinkers, these kinds of prices are extremely tough to justify.

It is certainly not an easy adjustment to make, going from a dollar per bottle to two or four times that amount. After years of writing about beer and glorifying some of the most expensive brews sold on this continent, even I have the occasional qualm about the prices I pay for certain beers. It is an attitude adjustment of a very high order, admittedly, but a necessary one nonetheless.

One easy way you can deal with your personal "sticker shock" is to change the way you drink beer. Unlike the standardized commercial lagers that are brewed for "drinkability," premium beers call for a little time to be savored and enjoyed, rather than guzzled cold. Obviously, this does not apply to all beers — best bitters, for example, are immensely pleasurable by the pint — but the more expensive ones will generally be those brewed for quiet consideration, and by enjoying them slowly in sips, much as you would a fine wine, you will definitely maximize your value for the dollar. After all, where a beer at five dollars a bottle might seem a little steep, a similarly sized bottle of wine is a bargain at twice the price, especially if that wine (beer) is a world classic!

The second necessary attitude adjustment will be to cast aside every preconception you have about beer. If you are like most residents of this continent, that will include the ideas that beer always needs to be served at cold temperatures, that lagers normally have light, sweet flavors and that beer does not have an aftertaste. Aside from being flat-out misconceptions, these prejudices will severely hamper your beer-enjoyment potential.

The importance of rejecting the beer-based mythology of North America lies at the feet of the wealth of beer styles you may encounter in the wild world of microbrewing. Can you imagine, for example, your reaction to a rave review of Pyramid Apricot Ale, flavored with the actual fruit, if you held these antiquated beer beliefs? Or your response to a story about a "winter warmer" like Geary's Hampshire Special Ale that spoke of its being a robust beer designed for quiet, fireside contemplation on a January eve when the winds are whistling and the snow is falling? You might well think the beer world had gone mad.

Truthfully, some brews will be sweet, occasionally very sweet, but others will be quite bitter or even somewhat sour. Some should be served cold whereas others are more suited to cellar- or room-temperature consumption. And as far as the aftertaste goes, well, that bizarre concept is a pure fabrication, created by some advertising agency commissioned to sell a beer that had no aftertaste. The bottom line is that beers come in all sorts of colors, styles and tastes; understanding this is the starting point for beer enjoyment.

With monetary limitations and false preconceptions shunted aside, what comes next?

START ME UP

If you are a microbrewery veteran who has supped your fill of bocks and barley wines and Scotch ales and spice beers, you may wish to skip this section and move on to the next, but then again, you may not. This section is a voyage of discovery, and it can be as informative and enlightening or as whimsical and entertaining as you want it to be, so even the committed microbrew fan can have fun with this trip to brews unknown.

The greatest advantage available to today's beer explorer is the comparative wealth of written material now on the market in the form of books, magazines and newspapers. The fact that you are reading this book is proof that you've discovered part of this written equation, but you may not be aware of the numerous resources available to you, ready for the taking! Magazines and brewspapers can now be commonly found at many bookstores, newsstands, home-brew shops or local watering holes (see Appendix II for a list of titles) and they aren't going to break the bank, either — the brewspapers are, in most cases, gratis. These are tremendous resources and, when they do cost you money, you can actually chalk up the expense as an investment in future savings because these publications will forewarn you about bad or mediocre beer.

When I began getting fascinated by beer, the only book widely available was Michael Jackson's *World Guide to Beer* (1982). As good as it was, and Jackson's subsequent books are, the experience was akin to attempting to earn a B.A. with a single textbook. Fortunately, I had the added benefit of working for two Belgians at the time and they helped and encouraged me immeasurably. You, on the other hand, have no need of Belgian employers because there now exists a veritable treasure trove of beer books on the shelves of your local bookstore, with more arriving almost weekly. Many of these books and periodicals are listed at the back of this book, but my advice with respect to reading material is the same as my advice on beer: keep your eyes open.

FROM BOOKSTORE TO BEER STORE

Now, what's a good read without a good beer to accompany it? So, the time has now come to head on down to your local beer emporium and pick up a few bottles.

But what to start with? True, there is much from which to choose, but seeing as you are beginning what will likely be a long voyage of beer discovery, there is no reason to get overenthusiastic right off the bat. Try starting with a selection of four beers: one that is of a style you are familiar with (lager or amber ale), one that is an offshoot of that style (German pils or British pale ale), one that looks like nothing you would ever think of drinking (fruit beer or oatmeal stout) and one that has the sharpest packaging in the shop. The reasoning behind this particular quartet of brews will be explained as we go along.

After you have taken the beers home and chilled them appropriately — ales, stouts, porters and the like at cellar temperature and lagers and wheat beers 15 to 30 minutes out of the fridge — open and sample each one with just a taste or two. Use clear glasses (wineglasses are great) and take a moment to appreciate the aroma before you sip. Take care not to prejudge a beer; dark brews won't necessarily taste "dark" and light-colored beers may not taste like anything you have ever encountered. Enjoy the beers on their own merits and look for flavors that you may not have expected to find in a beer. Take your time; there can be no rushing exploration.

Now ask yourself what you have just tasted. If you liked them all, figure out what it was that you enjoyed more about one than another. If there was one you didn't like, or if you hated all four, what was it that you disliked? If you have some books, magazines or brewspapers handy, look them up in those publications and try to find out whether or not they tasted the way they were meant to taste. Was it the aroma that put you off? The color? Close your eyes and have someone hand you a glass containing an unidentified brew. Did it taste the same when you couldn't see its color? Now try the experiment with your eyes closed and your nose plugged.

What you have been doing is cataloguing your likes and dislikes. You already knew that you liked at least one beer similar to the first beer you picked (the one of a familiar style), but you had to find out whether it was the style you enjoyed or the habit of drinking it. As for the related style, there you were testing the flexibility of your drinking habits and discovering whether this might be the place to start your beer-tasting journeys. The outrageous beer was picked to establish the parameters of your search; if you liked it, then you are wide open to trying anything next time, but if you hated it, you will want to pull back the boundaries, at

TOOTHPASTE — THE SCOURGE OF
THE BEER TASTER

One of the most difficult problems facing a beer taster is the constant struggle to maintain an unadulterated palate. Foods, spices, drinks and even other beers can ruin a taster's palate as quickly as you can say "garlic bread" and, even for a casual beer lover, render all beery judgments invalid. The worst offender of all, however, is that mint marauder, the poisoner of palates and toxin of taste itself — toothpaste.

Designed to clean teeth and freshen breath, it should come as no surprise that toothpastes of all sorts stick to the taste buds like glue and require hours before they release their iron grip. The challenge for a beer lover unwilling to compromise his or her dental hygiene, then, becomes one of speeding the release of the toothpaste's hold.

There are several methods of expunging the taste of the paste from one's palate, but they all require a little help from Father Time, for no flavor in the world is going to overpower toothpaste without leaving a strong memory of its own. One rather surprising palate refresher is coffee, a strong taste that will still require at least an hour or so to fade but is guaranteed to overpower toothpaste. Another method of neutralizing the paste is to meet it with a contradictory flavor such as apple, orange or grapefruit juice, thus producing a singularly nasty taste experience but one that will fade more quickly than the toothpaste alone. And a third toothpaste squasher is fresh bread and lots of it, an agent that will still take a while to work and may fill you up in the meantime, but is sure to win the day.

least temporarily. And the "design" beer, the one with the slick packaging, was chosen to add an element of chance to the affair. If you got lucky, you enjoyed a great-looking and great-tasting beer, otherwise you got a fine illustration of the power of label design.

Taking the rest of the afternoon — I did say this would take all afternoon, didn't I? — slowly finish your four beers one at a time, including the ones you didn't like. At the end of the experience, repeat those questions you posed earlier to see if you like the brews more after you have become accustomed to them. Don't be surprised if you find you do like them the second time around; some great beers just take a little time to grow on you. Often, even for experienced tasters, what began as a questionable call finishes as an impressive beer.

After repeating this process a few times and reading a bit more, you should be well on your way to some very satisfying beer appreciation. Of course, the more you experiment and read, the harder it will be to find what you consider to be "weird styles" and you will become less inclined to choose a beer based solely on its label, so you'll have to adjust the format a bit as you go. Just avoid the tempting trap of repeatedly revisiting a favored beer and you should find that your voyage of discovery is actually quite smooth sailing.

As you will no doubt find, the hardest part of learning about beer is conditioning yourself to let your tastes evolve with each new brew after a lifetime of generic lagers. As tough as this part of the process can be, it is also the most rewarding. When I was first starting on my beery road, someone gave me a brew that I thought was just awful, wretched stuff. Why, I wondered, would anyone want to drink this stuff?

The beer? It was only the world-classic Belgian ale, Duvel!

THE FIVE STEPS TO BEER ENJOYMENT

I was a beer lover long before I became a beer writer and my preoccupation with the discovery of new brews has provided me with many an hour of great pleasure and relaxation. During that time, I have consistently relied on the following five basic points of beer enjoyment to guide my beery adventures. Some of these may seem a trifle repetitive after reading the above section, but I believe that they are worth emphasizing.

1. Try everything you can get your hands on

When you are out for the evening, either at a bar or a friend's place, sample several beers instead of sticking to only one brand for the evening. Many multi-tap bars and brewpubs will offer small glasses of draft for tasting at bargain prices, so take advantage of their generosity, and bear in mind that bottled brews can always be split between two or more tasters. Just remember that the goal here is to sample many beers, not drink ravenously of each, and don't forget to tip the bar staff accordingly for their extra effort.

The same principle can also be applied to beer purchased for home consumption. Instead of buying a six-pack of one brand, select a bottle or two of several different beers. The obvious advantage of doing your beer tasting at home is that you can space out your beers over days instead of hours, and by buying different brews each time you visit the store, you can be assured of always having a variety of beers available. Sure, not all of them will be great and some may even be bad, but at least you will be able to say that you have tried them!

2. While traveling, always look for the local beer fare

This should be the most basic tenet of every beer aficionado, yet its logic sometimes escapes even the most dedicated beerophiles. With brewing becoming increasingly regionalized, there is a good chance that the beer you see on a trip may never make it as far as your hometown, so it makes sense to try it while you have the opportunity. This may require a little sleuthing—local breweries are sometimes so small that not even the natives are aware of them—but a knowledgeable concierge or bartender, or a local entertainment guide, can shorten your quest.

As one who frequently travels solo, I have found that not only do such beer hunts help me in my business, they also keep me occupied and leave less time for loneliness. Naturally, I still miss my wife terribly while on the road, but somehow a good beer and a friendly bartender in a pleasant setting makes the whole situation just that much more tolerable.

3. Think about your beer

Drinking beer is easy, thinking about beer requires a bit more commitment; where the act of drinking involves nothing more than raising a glass to your lips and swallowing, thinking entails contemplation and consideration. There are many facets of enjoyment in a beer and, in order to explore them all, you need to take some time to peruse all of its elements in a leisurely fashion, from color to aroma to taste and aftertaste. True, there will be times when you wish only to enjoy a good beer without dwelling on it too extensively, but there will be more times—and more rewarding times—when the quiet appreciation of a beer will yield the greatest satisfaction. It's a little more work than just drinking, but the rewards are worth it!

4. Involve all of your friends

This is very important; drinking on your own, like dining alone, is depressing at the best of times and it becomes even more so when you unearth a great new beer and have no one available to share in your discovery. Getting your friends interested in craft beer, then, rewards you with tasting partners and gives them the benefits of a world of beer tastes and treasures—*your world*. It also opens the door to beer-tasting parties, brewpub crawls, beer dinners and general group-based beer enjoyment.

A potential side benefit to converting your friends to craft beer is that once they have discovered the joys of the beer world, they, too, will go beer hunting whenever they travel and, out of gratitude for your beery guidance, perhaps even bring back unfamiliar bottles for you to taste. For this reason, it is particularly important to focus your beer missionary energies on friends who travel a lot in their business.

5. Get informed and stay informed

The craft beer industry is a nebulous thing, constantly changing and evolving as it grows bigger and stronger, and it is for this reason that reliable information becomes your most potent ally in your search for ever better beers. If there is one absolute truth in the beer enjoyment game, it is that you can't taste beers that you don't know exist.

Books, especially beer guides, are a good start in your beer information quest, but they are by their very nature limited in how current their information can be. It is best, then, to supplement your library with beer magazines and brewspapers. You may also find it beneficial to lobby your local newspaper for a regular beer column or, at least, for more frequent mention of developments on the local brewing front. After all, why should wine get all the good press?

FESTIVAL HOPPING

If a formal beer hunt is not your cup of tea — or pint of ale — yet you still want to get in on the craft brewing renaissance, there are a few shortcuts available. One such beery bypass is that new breed of North American consumer show: the beer festival.

Beer fests take many forms and their numbers are growing yearly. At the time of the very first Great American Beer Festival in 1982, it was quite literally alone in a field dominated by wine fairs and the occasional home-brewing competition. By the end of 1994, however, the beer festival had turned into an industry all its own and there are now beer fests large and small occurring in virtually every region on the continent.

From gala affairs attracting thousands of people to simple evening tastings at local bars, beer festivals offer beer explorers unparalleled opportunities to taste brands from all across their region, the country or the world. And, perhaps more important, these brews can be tasted side by side with their competitors and peers, thus affording the patron a chance to compare and contrast different examples of similar styles. On a continent where beer drinkers are increasingly educating themselves about the full potential of beer's flavors, a beer festival provides the ultimate classroom.

But as a good teacher would not enter the schoolhouse without a lesson plan, neither should the beer aficionado attend a festival without a course of action. Because whether there are fifty or five hundred or fifteen hundred brews available for tasting, you simply will not be able to get to them all, guaranteed. The only way to ensure that you do not miss rare or unusual brews, or beers that you particularly want to taste for one reason or another, is to have a game plan.

NORTH AMERICAN BEER FESTIVALS

This list indicates but a few of the dozens of beer festivals held all across the continent. Look for one in your neck of the woods or plan your travels around one of the many regional fests.

Great American Beer Festival—Held in Denver during October, this is the largest beer festival in the world in terms of brands offered. Expect well over 1,000 different brews.

Oregon Brewers Festival—Portland-based and open-air, this July festival attracts more beer lovers than any other on the continent. Each brewer is limited to a single, draft brand, so breweries will showcase only their best.

KQED Beer and Food Festival—A benefit for the San Francisco public broadcaster, it is the oldest beer fest in California. Both domestic and international brands abound at this July event and fine food is supplied by local restaurants and grocers.

Boston Brewers Festival—The unusual aspect of this May festival is that it brings together breweries from both the United States and Canada. For easterners, it's one of the largest fests going.

Victoria Microbrewery Festival—This British Columbia event is the largest of a fairly sparse Canadian contingent of beer festivals. Normally it is held in October and features microbrews from Canada and the United States.

Southeastern Microbrewers Invitational—With its 1994 premier, this April event marked the coming of major beer festivals to the southeastern United States. It is held in Durham, North Carolina.

Festibière de Chambly—While yet to debut at the time of writing, this five-day combination trade and consumer show promises to be a grand September event. As the name indicates, it will be held in the Montreal suburb of Chambly.

As festival guides are generally unavailable in advance of the actual event, your planning will necessitate a brief pause for organization and orientation just after you enter the festival grounds. So, once you have gained admittance, pick up a program, grab yourself a nearby sample of something light—by all means, do not start off with a smoked or chili beer!—and find a quiet corner where you can peruse the guide.

There are several strategies you may wish to adopt at a festival, and the one you pick will depend upon your priorities. You may wish to visit specific breweries, for example, in which case you should find and mark them on your guide map, or perhaps you would prefer to examine a specific beer style. In the latter case, you should obviously find all the examples of that style in your guide and, because most people will start at the front of the program and work to the back, you might want to try visiting them in counter-alphabetical order—you will be surprised at the crowds you avoid that way. If there are multiple styles you wish to visit, be sure to proceed from lightest to heaviest so that your palate is not exhausted by the time you hit the wheat beers, and if flavored beers are in your plans, make especially sure to leave them until the end.

Whatever strategy you choose, you can be sure that it will serve you better than random roaming and tasting. Moreover, a strategy will allow you to better time your festival experience so that you will not find yourself madly running about trying to grab ten tastes within the final ten minutes.

Beer festival education is not confined merely to tasting, however. These events also offer rare opportunities to talk to the people behind the beer. Beer "celebrities" such as British author Michael Jackson, the Boston Beer Company's Jim Koch and Pete Slosberg of Pete's Wicked Ale fame frequently make appearances at such events and brewers and brewery owners can often be found lurking around their respective booths, as well. Taking the time and opportunity to speak with these people will dramatically help you in your beer journeys, *and* give you something to brag about to your friends. And from brewer to writer to investor to sales representative, beer people are among the most sociable and talkative you will ever meet.

THE SOCIABLE BEER

I have frequently heard wine writers and vintners alike say that after a hard day making or tasting wine, they often like nothing more than to relax with a beer. Likewise, beer writers and brewers will note that following a hard day at their work, they like to kick back with a glass of... beer! There is a reason for this, and it has nothing to do with the relative sophistication of the two drinks or the idea that beer people cannot fully appreciate wine; beer is every bit as complex as its cousin of the vine and many people associated with the brewing industry, myself included, are great admirers of the grape. No, this situation has to do with the sheer sociability of beer.

VIVE LES TABLES DE MONTRÉAL

In Montreal, where I grew up, people know how to enjoy their beer. Every night in the city is a social night, from Monday to Sunday, and most afternoons qualify, as well. Life, as all Montrealers know, is meant to be lived and that means going out to the bars, the cafés and the clubs and meeting and socializing with your fellow city dwellers. It also usually means drinking beer.

Per capita, Montrealers are no more prodigious in their beer consumption than Torontonians or New Yorkers; where they differ is in the time they spend sipping their beer. In Montreal, beer is the ultimate social elixir and mixer.

An illustration of the Montreal attitude toward beer drinking — indeed that of most of Quebec — is evidenced by the time-honored table of choice in the province's licensed establishments: the one-foot-square beer table. This table, peculiar by most modern standards but still commonplace in Montreal, has room enough for an ashtray and four beer glasses, period. If you are really careful, you might be able to squeeze on five or six glasses, and maybe even find a corner on which to rest your elbow, but certainly nothing else. No briefcases open for business, no spreadsheets, no note-pads and definitely no cellular phones.

It is actually quite refreshing to find yourself seated at one of these tiny bar tables. For here is a table that has no use other than to hold your beer while you debate the pros and cons of government policy with your table-mates. It does not dominate the area and so allows you to move around the room with ease, changing places as the whim strikes, and it is so simple that it cannot possibly support any pretensions. And you can check your ideas about personal space at the door, for this table is too small for such petty considerations.

We do not often dwell on whether or how the furniture around us affects our sociability, but I believe that it does and to a great degree. Bar and tavern owners in Quebec obviously agree with me, or they would not have stuck with this ridiculously small but incredibly sociable table for all these years.

In his appetizingly eloquent food column for *The Globe and Mail* newspaper, writer and editor John Allemang makes the following poignant observation: "Small servings invariably seem precious and invite a silent, reverential gaze. The best and loosest conversation comes — don't ask me why — when there is plenty of food on the plate."

As true as this is in terms of dining, it has equal veracity when applied to drink. The larger portions in which beer is generally served, twelve ounces or a pint, dwarf smaller cocktails such as martinis or Cuba libres and make six-ounce servings of wine seem miserly. This, coupled with the casual nature of most beers, makes beer a perfect drink for on-your-feet socializing or across-the-table debating. If you doubt this, head down to your favorite local bar or pub to see for yourself.

After grabbing a seat with a good view of the entire establishment, take stock of the inhabitants of the room, how they are behaving and what they are drinking. If your bar is like most bars, the most animated conversations will be coming from the beer drinkers among the clientele. This is not because they are necessarily more interesting than the wine or spirits drinkers, although they may be, it is just that their conviviality is enhanced by the type of drink they are enjoying. Rather ironically, it is beer rather than the higher-alcohol wines and spirits that seems to best relax people when they are in a social setting, and this effect is purely a function of the way beer is held, carried and consumed.

BEER AND GENDER

While you are at the bar making observations, there is another matter into which you may wish to delve, although it will only be observable in a bar with a decent beer selection. It is, in a way, the single most liberating consequence of the craft beer renaissance and perhaps the most dramatic, too. For the first time in centuries, women are claiming beer as their own.

It may not seem like much of a development, but after decades of "Bud men" and "me and the boys and our 50" (the latter a longtime Labatt ad), the fact that craft beer has opened its arms to the female gender represents no small turning point. You can see it at the bars and you can see it at the beer festivals; craft beer has (mercifully) become a genderless drink.

I first observed the female part of the craft brewing equation at the 1992 Great American Beer Festival. While I had certainly noticed that many women were entering the industry on the production side, I had not taken stock of the role women played on the consumption end of things. At the GABF, however, it was an unavoidable fact: women in twos, threes or larger groups were to be found all around the festival hall, enjoying their beer and talking about it amongst themselves. And with nary a stereotypically beer-bellied boyfriend in sight.

The female role in the profile of the average craft beer consumer has not gone unnoticed by the industry, either. Microbreweries are now keenly aware that women constitute a significant portion of their market and they are responding appropriately. Most brewpubs, or at least those that emphasize the quality of their beer, present female-friendly environments devoid of the trappings of the male domain, and microbreweries take care to avoid any hints of sexism in their advertising. In the 1990s, no smart small brewery owner is about to ignore up to half of his or her customer base.

If the gender factor in craft brewing is one that is worth developing further, John Hall is the man who is developing it. Hall is the owner of the Goose Island Brewing Company in Chicago and, by my experience, one very observant man. For it was John who took my suggestion that women were enjoying craft beer as much as men and enhanced it one step further. Women, he said, were not only enjoying good beer, they were more experimental about doing so than men.

John's observation, made in a semisecluded corner of his brewpub, was that women were more likely than guys to try darker, heavier and stranger brews. The inclination to try new things, he maintained, seemed to come more easily to women than men and it showed in the beers they chose, or at least it did at Goose Island.

To illustrate his point, we walked out to the packed bar area and observed the many bi-gender groups drinking at the pub. Sure enough, at almost every table, most men were sipping lighter lagers, while the majority of women were enjoying darker and heavier brews. That one night, at least, the women certainly seemed to be in a much more experimental state of mind than the men.

Since that time, I have observed this practice on numerous occasions, but have seen the theory fail many times, as well. As much as that side of the equation calls for further research, the pivotal role that women are now playing in the development of the microbrewing industry is beyond dispute. For the consumer, this refreshing development means that men and women have finally found a common beverage bond.

WHETHER GOING OUT...

With its secure status as an eminently sociable beverage for both men and women, beer is obviously the perfect beverage around which to build an evening with friends. And if building a night out around beer sounds like an odd concept, you may be missing out on one of beer's great unifying strengths.

Since humans first conceived of the days of the week, one question has plagued societies past and present, near and far: What to do on Saturday night. It has perplexed philosophers (Socrates: "I know nothing except the fact of my ignorance, and that includes what to do Saturday night"), playwrights (Shakespeare: To be, or not to be, and what to do Saturday night — those are the questions") and politicians (Kennedy: "Ask not what your country can do for you, ask what you want to do this Saturday"). It is the eternal dilemma and, in beer, we may finally have found an answer.

Getting a group of friends together for a night on the town is never easy; some people want to shoot some pool, others would rather go dancing and another contingent would prefer to see a band. You might be able to get everyone to agree to dinner, but that would entail either a lot of work preparing a meal yourself or a significant cash layout for dinner at a restaurant, neither of which is terribly appealing when a large crowd is involved. The solution, then, is a beer hunt.

Beer hunting, I must admit, is not my idea; it belongs to writer Michael Jackson, who is also known as The Beer Hunter and whose hunt has extended to the four corners of the globe. Of course, your hunt need not range so far afield, but given the right conditions and circumstances, it can be equally enlightening.

The local beer hunt is essentially a focused pub crawl. You begin by assembling a group of friends and acquaintances, from four to 40, and selecting a bar or pub from which to begin your explorations. It will be important that your friends understand the beery orientation of the night, but also that they not dwell on the fact, because beer hunting is only fun as long as it does not become a grail-like pursuit — keep it mellow and non-judgmental at all times.

Beginning at brewpub or beer bar number one, encourage your mates to experiment with different brews and to sip and sample from one another's glasses (hey, we're all friends here, right?). This will likely be the only point where such prompting will be necessary, as people will become naturally predisposed toward unusual beers as they taste more of what beer has to offer. In the due course of time, sociability will take over, with beer rising only occasionally to the surface of conversation, and the night will assume a convivial tone of enjoyment amongst friends. This is where you, as the organizer, will have to make a decision: Do you stay and let the natural karma of the night run its course, or is it time to shepherd your friends to the next stop?

If you decide that reinvigoration is necessary, then allow a good 30 minutes to get your crew together and move them onward. Nowhere in nature does the physics law of a body at rest staying at rest apply more than in a comfortable bar, so it will take some time to prompt everyone to action; be firm, but stay casual about the whole thing. Your next stop should be within a short distance of your first, preferably walking distance. Once there, the intrigue of a new group of brews from which to choose will likely stimulate your group and beer will become the dominant topic of conversation once again. Flow with it, have fun with it, but don't let it become oppressive; if people are obsessing about the brews, a change of conversation is definitely in order.

If your crew numbers more than ten, your third stop will be your last and you will be lucky to have taken such a group that far. By the time you reach this bar, beer should be incidental to all but the most hard-core aficionados and the social aspect of the night will have taken over. Don't force the issue now; let people enjoy themselves and their beers and watch the rest of the night unfold. You have done your work and your friends will thank you.

A successful beer hunt will yield several beneficial results: one, beer will have proven to be a catalyst to get together a group of friends, many of whom might otherwise have been difficult to organize; two, everyone will have tasted at least one or two brews with which they were unfamiliar and will have advanced their beer knowledge — thanks to you; and three, no one will have consumed more than a moderate amount of alcohol, partly because the movement from bar to bar precludes heavy drinking and partly because tasting and gulping are incompatible. In total, it should have been a very enjoyable evening.

...OR STAYING IN

As much fun as going out for beer hunting can be, it can be equally pleasurable to pursue your explorations in the comforts of your own home. Such indoor beer hunting generally takes one of two forms — the beer tasting or the beer dinner.

Actually, to describe these gustatory adventures as beer hunting is a trifle misleading, seeing as your actual hunt will have taken place earlier. But for your guests, these occasions will indeed be true beer hunts.

The first step for either a beer tasting or dinner will, of course, have to be the accumulation of your brews. This may be accomplished all in one shot if you are lucky enough to have a good beer store in your vicinity, otherwise it will necessitate more, and possibly considerably more, effort on your part. It could, in fact, end up being a process that will take weeks or months to complete, depending on how many brews you want and how finicky you are about which brands you choose. Normally, however, a fair selection can generally be picked up without too much fuss in most cities and a good many towns.

For the beer tasting, you will probably want at least six to ten different brews, and unless you anticipate a huge crowd, two or three bottles of each brand should suffice. (It must be emphasized here that these recommendations are for social tastings only; serious, evaluatory tastings will require much more rigidity and should never, in my opinion, exceed a maximum of six different brews.) If you have access to a computer—and who doesn't these days?—you may wish to work up a scoring sheet for your guests using a scale of anywhere from 1 to 10 or 1 to 50. Whatever your rating system, you want your guests to be scoring the appearance, aroma, taste and overall impression they have of each beer, with the weighing of points roughly divided into 50 percent for flavor and more or less equal amounts for everything else. (For some reason, the assignment of numbers is a very comforting action for anyone engaged in the evaluation of beer, wine or virtually any other comestible and so the opportunity to rate and rank will be welcomed by your tasters. Personally, I have always preferred to emphasize descriptions rather than numerical designations, but this intimidates some people who doubt their own descriptive abilities, usually without cause.)

In setting up your tasting, you will want to have each beer chilled to an appropriate temperature and set out in an attractive display. The kitchen- or dining-room table is always a good place at which to set up, and you can add a touch of class by using a white tablecloth and liberally distributing (unscented) candles around the room. A pitcher of water for glass rinsing and palate cleansing is recommended and you will want to make sure that you have snack food available, but nothing so salty, spicy, oily or overly pungent that it will brutalize the taste buds of your guests. If you want to be particularly fastidious, you can even match your snack foods to your beers, but a selection of mild to medium cheeses, breads and perhaps some grapes or pâté will suffice nicely.

Furnish each of your guest tasters with a clear wineglass and a separate glass of water and invite them to proceed at their leisure, taking a two- to three-ounce portion of each beer in turn. Because this is a social occasion, the mood should remain light and friendly, so make sure that no one feels obligated to engage in in-depth ruminations about every single beer. A simple reminder that the evaluation is for their own individual use should be enough to ensure that no such intimidation is felt.

If you have been able to secure a quantity of each beer that was involved in the tasting, you can offer your guests a chance to enjoy more of their favorite brew after they finish their evaluations. Otherwise, have beers of equal quality available for post-tasting consumption—it is a big letdown to be entranced by great beers for part of the evening and subjected to poor ones for the remainder of the night.

You may discuss the beer after your tasting bottles have been exhausted, and you likely will for a time, but such talk is entirely unnecessary unless it is specifically desired by your guests. Even the best of us sometimes just want to drink our beer without thinking too much about it!

THE BEER DINNER

Like the casual tasting, the beer dinner will require as much of you as you are willing to put into it. Conceivably, this could range from a two-course meal of pasta followed by gelato, with appropriate accompanying beers, to a feast of five, six or more courses, each matched to one or several different brews. If you want it to be complicated, a beer dinner can certainly fit that bill.

For a first beer dinner, I would recommend three or four courses with a single, matching beer per dish. This way you will neither put too much pressure on yourself — there is no fun in preparing a meal if it causes a nervous breakdown — nor will it intimidate your guests. Once again, the social aspect should be paramount in any beer entertaining and anything that detracts from that element will necessarily also detract from the enjoyment of the beers.

In planning your menu, you may find it helpful to use some of the recipes furnished in Chapter 6, or you may wish to refer to any of the beer cookbooks that are listed in Appendix II. Whatever your choice, the beers you select to complement your food should be well thought out — you do want to astonish your dinner guests, after all. You will also want to bear in mind that, like the cardinal rule about never using an ingredient twice within a single meal, you should not present the same beer twice during the same dinner. There is certainly enough variety within the world of beer to accommodate even the most extravagant of meals without repetition.

Arrange your dishes so that the accompanying beers proceed from the lightest to the heaviest, with rare exceptions. One example of such a deviation would be if you were to serve raw oysters as an appetizer, a dish that would beg for an accompanying stout and leave you with precious few beer styles from which to choose for the rest of your courses. Use your better judgment, and try to avoid such incongruities as wheat beer following a rich and heavy barley wine.

While you will want to use local, in-season ingredients in your cooking, there is no reason to feel obliged to use local beer fare for your matches. It is true that the freshness of such beers will, in general, tend to be more reliable than that of beers that have been shipped across the country or around the world, but this is no reason to exclude the many great brews that fall into the latter group. Just make sure that you check freshness codes if any are available, look for any inappropriate cloudiness or sediment in the bottle and, above all, buy from a reliable and knowledgeable retailer.

Now it is time to sit down at the table! Owing to their preconceptions about how beer is meant to be consumed, your guests may expect to receive a full bottle of each brew with every course, but it is your job to disappoint them — for their benefit. Because beer is carbonated, it will fill the stomach more quickly than still beverages and may contribute to a bloated sensation long before one is deserved, so your eating companions will thank you at the end of the meal if you limit their intake to a half bottle or less of each beer.

Following John Allemang's advice, present your guests with healthy plates of good, flavorful food, for these are the kinds of servings that best reflect the personality of beer and the kind of sociability you strive for in any entertainment setting. As any chef knows, this need not mean that your china must be piled high with food, but that the aura of plenty is created at the place setting. Put candles on the table, along with specialty breads, relishes, soft butter, seasonings and whatever else may tickle your fancy. Cover, rather than pile, the plate with food, and sprinkle herbs or pepper around the exposed portions of the dish. And bearing in mind the importance of color, employ garnishes of parsley, paprika or peppercorns to liven up otherwise monotone dishes. There should, no, there *must* be a sense of joy to your table.

A beer dinner should never be staid. A sense of fun and enthusiasm must dominate the affair and priggish snobbery should be positively *verboten*. If you have done your homework as host, the beers will speak for themselves and indulgence, rather than evaluation, will become the dominant theme of the night. Good beer plus good food plus good company is one equation that will always add up to a good time, enjoyed by all.

ROMANCING THE HOP

No treatise on gastronomic enjoyment would be complete without a visit to the ultimate type of enjoyment; indeed, since time immemorial, taste and temptation have been inextricably linked. It was the taste of an apple, after all, that tempted Adam and Eve in the Garden of Eden—although I wouldn't be surprised to find that the legend has become distorted through the centuries and that it was actually a cider or apple ale that prompted the inevitable fall from grace. Taste, in its many luscious, savory and succulent forms, is as close as we humans can come to rapture with our clothes still on. And, yes, beer is one of those forms.

If you have any doubt about the relationship between taste and the more sensuous pleasures of the flesh, watch the couples dining in a fine restaurant some time. See their eyes light up as they savor some particularly juicy morsel, listen to the soft moans slipping from their lips as they embrace a new forkful of flavors, watch their bodies move as though aching to share food and partner in the same impossible mouthful. There is no need for blindfolded gustatory guessing games à la *9½ Weeks*; good food and drink is sexy by its very nature.

Beer, however, is seldom thought of as a terribly sensuous or romantic drink. This is, again, a slight on beer. For, while we may be more inclined to resort to wine when wooing would-be paramours, beer can fit the bill every bit as competently if given half a chance. In fact, beer may even perform better than wine in this regard, particularly if, as Mario D'Eer suggests in his *Guide de la Bonne Bière*, hops are an aphrodisiac! It would be nice if it were true, but even without such motivations being offered by the noble flower, beer can be as romantic as you wish it to be.

So much of romance is not what you do, but how you do it. So it follows that whereas a pint glass of bitter or an ordinary tumbler of pilsner will not be very romantic, a fluted glass filled with lipstick-pink cherry beer or a snifter of deep and mysterious barley wine will cast a very different glow on a firelit night. Likewise, bringing a six-pack of cans to a spring picnic will hardly endear you to a potential lover, but offer a shimmering sleeve of glistening white beer instead and see what a difference it will make!

Romance, however, is one thing and sensuality quite another; the sensuality of drink is embodied not in its container but in its taste. Complexities are important in any bedroom beer, as is a preferred serving temperature of cellar or warmer; frigid drinks do nothing for the libido, unless the thermometer has just exploded and the air conditioner sputtered its last gasp. Pick low-carbonation beers — no burping! — and something with gorgeous flavors that you can taste in each other's eyes. Pour small amounts so that you will need to refill the glasses more frequently and thus to stay close to your love, and sip and savor the nectars slowly.

Such sensuous imbibing elicits very powerful feelings of warmth and desire from even the most tentative partner, and the stunning sensations of taste, in the proper context, will perfectly and naturally lead to sensations of a similar, but, at the same time, quite different type. Just remember to put your glass down first.

CHAPTER 4

CELEBRATING
THE SEASONS

The millennium is divided into centuries, the centuries into decades, the decades into years; yet while each division functions nicely within the boundaries of tens, only the seasons refuse the dictatorship of the decimal. Why? Because the seasons are nature and nature suits itself, not us.

But as uncompromising as nature is, humankind has proven to be much less so, as we willingly adapt *our* cycles to suit the comings and goings of the seasons. We feel the joy and newness of spring, revel in the frivolity of summer, mark the fall with an unflinching return to more serious pursuits and celebrate the end of one year, and the birth of another, in the winter. Marvelously—miraculously!—we fall into the current of the seasons and seldom even attempt to swim against the tide. Nature, despite all of our denials, is us.

As a part of our seasonal adaptation, we adjust our eating schedules to suit the seasons, as well. Those of us who reside in northern climes instinctively beef up during the winter, indulging in hearty stews and similar comfort foods, while the summer brings to all a desire for lighter fare, including the literal fruits of the season and salads of many descriptions and, of course, the ubiquitous barbecue. In the fall, we celebrate the harvest by making use of all the fresh produce that wends its way to the shelves of our stores. Springtime's anticipatory feel compels us to look earthward for colors, any colors, with which to decorate the dull, winter hues that have dominated our plates for months.

Despite all of this conscious and subconscious gastronomic timetabling, however, North American beer drinkers seem, for the most part, to be content to sip the same brew or brews all year long, without any recognition of the extraneous conditions the seasons invoke. We are all too aware of the snow and ice and cold of winter until we set foot in a bar or restaurant, at which time we become oblivious to the cold and call for an icy lager. In spring, we watch the renewal of life, yet ignore the bodily call for something different in our glass. Our summer beer becomes an ice-cold "pop" instead of a satisfying and quenching experience, and our fall lager speaks nothing of the astounding transformations taking place outdoors.

It just doesn't make sense!

There is a natural current for beer enjoyment and riding it is nothing if not exhilarating. Beer styles exist for all seasons, and for very good reasons, and accepting and acknowledging this diversity and applicability is simply one more way to get the most out of your brew. Besides, ignoring the beery scheduling of the seasons is tantamount to ignoring nature itself, and we all know how far *that* will get us.

Spring

SEASON OF THE BOCK

Springtime is a time of growth and renewal, when buds appear on the trees, flowers begin to bloom and there is much joy to be found in the newness and endurance of life. Such as it is in nature, so, too, is it in the brewing business.

Each spring sees a volley of new brands and brews come onto the North American market, from wheats for the approaching summer months to spring bocks and various other, more eclectic, brews. There is very sound, practical motivation behind this, namely that spring represents a time when North Americans begin to think about drinking beer again and the market for beer, following its traditional winter dormancy, starts to flourish once more. What better time than spring to capture the public's attention with a new brand?

The emergence of these new brews provides a magnificent opportunity to experiment in and explore the world of beer, and for this reason, beer hunting is seldom better than in spring. In a sense, it is analogous to the attraction that zoos hold in the months of April, May and June, when the "zoo babies" make their public debut and people flock to ooh and aah at them. In the case of beer, those "babies" are spring bocks.

It remains, to my knowledge, undocumented, but the German town of Einbeck must surely have been the place of origin for the bock style. The second syllable of the town's name is pronounced by Bavarians as something roughly approximating "bock" and, according to beer sleuth Michael Jackson, the beers that made the town famous for its brewing in the fourteenth and fifteenth centuries were likely strong, dark, wheat-based brews—predecessors of the bottom-fermented beers we know today as bocks.

As the bock style evolved through the centuries, its traditional season became the spring, or perhaps that should read *one* of its traditional seasons. For the time of the bock varies quite dramatically around the world, with some breweries electing to unveil their bock in the fall, others choosing the winter and still others brewing the style all year long. In Bavaria, however, where they know a thing or two about beer, the dominant season remains the spring. There is even a German bock style, occasionally brewed in North America, called Maibock, literally "the bock of May."

The ideal season for bock exploration must surely be the spring, when new brands are emerging onto the market and the fall and winter bocks are still generally available. This is prime bock-hunting time, and woe unto the committed beer aficionado who misses it.

Bock hunting is a pursuit best suited to sizable groups of people, mainly because bocks are strong beers and any hunt worth its mandate will certainly unearth at least seven or eight of the ruby-colored gems—more than enough to put one or two tasters under the table. This being the case, "the more the merrier" should be your motto when setting out on your bock hunt.

It is my belief that bock hunting, or at least the tasting part of it, is best undertaken in the home. My reasons for this conclusion are threefold: one, few beer bars will have a strong enough selection of bocks to warrant an extended hunt; two, the home allows you a chance to select your own gastronomic accompaniment, and bocks marry so well with mildly pungent cheeses like gorgonzola and roquefort, the kind so few restaurants or bars elect to stock; and three, the richness of bocks and the long periods of maturation they require tend to place them among the pricier brews and that impact will be minimized if you buy them at the store. Some North American bocks to be on the lookout for include: Sierra Nevada Pale Bock, Brick Anniversary Bock, Samuel Adams Double Bock, Vancouver Island's Hermannator, any of the Stoudt bocks (there are four), New Glarus Uff-da Bock, Niagara Falls Eisbock, Brasal Bock, Heckler Dopple Bock and, even though it's actually an ale, the Sam Adams Triple Bock to finish the night.

The day of your bock hunt should offer classic, early-spring weather—warm and sunny but with a hint of crispness still in the air. You should begin in the late afternoon, with the shadows just creeping up and cooling things down, reminding us that winter's grip has not yet relented. Gather your friends in a room with an ample supply of windows, so that you all might watch the day recede while you enjoy your bocks.

Have your cheeses or other foods laid out on display and maybe even place a few daffodils in a vase in the corner. If you have a fireplace nearby, prepare for a fire in advance and light it when the last traces of the sun quietly slip below the horizon; remember, it's early spring and you can still get away with such things. Now, pour your beers and toast the arrival of spring in a celebration of the regeneration of life, then continue your tasting and regenerate yourself a bit.

APRIL SHOWERS

If there is one weather effect that, more than any other, promotes reflective thought and contemplation, it is the spring rainstorm.

As the thunder rattles off in the distance and sheets of water cascade from the skies to form a rhythmic pattern of *slap, slap, slap* against the windows, memories tend to flood the brain like waves of water flooding the curbsides. We consider times past, joys felt, decisions made and loves won and lost, and even when we try to reject the lure of the storm, we still find ourselves drawn unceasingly under its spell.

For some, the hypnotic powers of the spring storm cast a raw shadow. They feel themselves submerged in a torrent of emotion and find that the flood only washes away the superficial mental barriers to reveal the raw edges of regrets, suffering and agitations past. To add alcohol of any sort to this tumultuous brew of emotion is only to invite sorrow.

Those who are able to feel joy in the spring rain, however, find incomparable opportunities for glad reflection and the celebration of achievement, whether large or small, earthshaking or devoutly personal. The rain frees the mind to wander among individual glories. And what better place to stroll among such victories than in the warm, familiar setting of your favorite pub.

The word *pub* is used to describe an astounding number of different types of establishments these days, and appears to have lost whatever descriptive meaning it may have once possessed. The owners of bars clad exclusively in neon and chrome now refer to their premises as pubs, with absolutely no apparent sense of the inappropriateness of the term and, in isolated cases, the word has even been used to describe certain brews or even their packaging, as in Boddington's Pub Ale or Pub Draught Guinness.

A true pub, however, should reflect the origins of the word — a short form of "public house" — and be a comfortable place that conveys a feeling of familiarity and warmth, even when visiting for the very first time on a cold, winter day. To my mind, at least, there should be ample amounts of wood and other natural fibers used in its construction and what most bars and restaurants would call decor should, in the case of a pub, be merely an *appearance*, devoid of any pretense or clever design, leaving no question as to its "pub-ness." And, perhaps most of all, a pub should have best bitter on tap.

Bitter is to a true pub as olive oil is to a trattoria, an essential component without which the tone of the place is irrevocably altered. Partly due to the social qualities of a good bitter and partly owing to the common British origins of both beer and pub, a fine ale like a Wellington County Arkell Best Bitter, a Wynkoop ESB or a Vermont Pub and Brewery Dogbite Bitter is the life's blood of a fine pub, regardless of whether or not it is the most popular brew sold on the premises. The point is that those who *know*, know to drink it.

Bitter is also the beer that lends itself best to those quiet, rainy afternoons in April and May, when the storms have come and brought with them the thrill of memories. That is the time to venture out to your local pub, order up a pint of the "best" and couple the reminiscences with the fresh, foresty feel of a good bitter. It is an emotional cocktail as good as any devised by humankind through the centuries and when you lower your glass following the final sip and prepare to leave to walk among the already evaporating puddles on the sidewalks, you may be surprised to find yourself counting your blessings along with your change.

OUT ON THE PATIO

Springtime imbibing needn't take place indoors, though. For the rains will eventually stop and the sun will shine and pasty white northerners will emerge from their air-fed cocoons to celebrate the beauties of the season; the artist's palette of colorful flowers, the lush greens of young grass and the brilliant blues of the vernal sky. What better reason to enjoy the outdoors?

As with most blessings, however, the bountiful beauty of spring is mixed with a curse; the allergic suffering endured by so many poor souls, myself included. Sure, we make valiant attempts to enjoy spring to the maximum, to walk in the fields among the new grasses (*achoo!*), to run with the children among the flowering groves (*achoo, achoo!*) and to revel in the rebirth of nature (*ACHOO!*). But we fail, and end up retreating indoors where we know our nasal trauma will be reduced and our sore, watering eyes will be able to rest.

But even the springtime-challenged deserve a chance to enjoy the outdoor glories of the season now and then, and in most cases, that opportunity can be provided most ably by the bar patio.

Whether it is called a patio or a terrace, garden or sidewalk café, the patio is the great springtime refuge of the allergic and nonallergic alike. For those of the former persuasion, the normally concrete footings of the patio provide a largely inorganic environment where the histamines exuded by young foliage should be in relatively short supply and, for the latter group, the patio provides a site for the simultaneous and legal enjoyment of both the outdoors and a beer. It is indeed springtime luxury.

The patio peaks in mid-to-late spring instead of the summer or fall, because that is when it is possible to enjoy its benefits all day long, from the warm but not steaming summer-like daylight hours to the coolness of the night, bereft of autumn's chill. Although I have witnessed Torontonians flock to patios as early as March or April, it is apparent that this is done only as an instinctive reaction to warmer weather, the blissful and unabashed enjoyment of patios does not fully begin until late May or June.

The choice of the best beer for patio-based imbibing is a bit of a nebulous proposition. Most important, you want nothing that will remind you of the winter so recently past, so no stouts, porters or strong ales need be admitted for consideration. The heat is not yet intense enough to warrant summer lagers and wheats, so that eliminates two other categories, and you may have already had your fill of the season's bocks, so they can be set aside, as well. It seems as though there is precious little left!

The answer to this odd dilemma can be found in the attitude of the season. For spring is a time of rolling with the weather, following the patterns of cloud, sun and rain and adjusting accordingly, and patio living is nothing if not a mirror of this. Your beer choice, then, should similarly roll with the seasonal movement of the brewing industry and reflect its timetable. In other words, when on the patio, it makes sense to select the new or seasonal brands that the industry in general loves to parade in the spring, regardless of what style they may be.

If this sounds like a cavalier recommendation, it is only because it is. But then, that is the way spring should be, especially for those of us who labor indoors all winter and wish only to be set free from its confines when the warmer spring months finally arrive. It is a time to be uncritical and experimental, and the mandarins of the beer business know that, so you might as well sit back and make the most of it. On the patio.

Summer

....

WHEAT BEER

In all of its American, Belgian and German incarnations, wheat beer has developed a reputation in North America as a summer beer, and it is a role it serves well. On a hot summer day, with the sun beating down relentlessly upon your back, there are few pleasures that compare with a nice, cold pint of well-made wheat.

Curiously, however, wheat beer has also developed several alternative personalities. In Oregon, for example, Widmer Brewing's yeast-dense Hefe-Weizen came from nowhere to become the brewery's surprise year-round best-seller, accounting for some 80 percent of Widmer's production. In Canada, Labatt markets a bottom-fermented, sweet-and-sour wheat beer, John Labatt Classic Wheat, as a tasty, if untraditional, fall specialty brand, purportedly brewed to celebrate the harvest. Recent years have seen a surge in the popularity of wheat bocks such as the sweet and somewhat fruity Pyramid Wheaten Bock from the Washington Hart Brewing, and, in what is perhaps the oddest incarnation of all, Niagara Falls Brewing applies the "wheat beer" tag to their 8.5% alcohol by volume Maple Wheat, a stunningly complex brew flavored with maple syrup and pure maple extract.

But still, the balanced banana, clove and light citrus of a weizen or the gentle spiciness of a wit are tough to beat when the weather warms and northern folk like myself emerge from their winter hibernation. When added to this ferocious pleasure are the charms of a brewpub patio, the combination proves almost impossible to resist, which is one reason, I believe, that wheats thrive more in the continent's northlands than in the always-balmy south.

There are exceptions, of course: the Celis Brewery's Celis White from Texas must surely be considered the finest Belgian-style wheat in North America and, indeed, one of the top wits in the world, and the Market Street Wheat from Nashville's Bohannon Brewing, while not in the same grandiose class as the Celis, is nonetheless quite pleasant and immensely drinkable. For the most part, however, one must look northward for choice wheat fare.

One such fine northern wheat comes from the Denison Brewing Company in Toronto, Ontario, a brewpub partially owned by Prince Luitpold of the Kaltenberg Brewery in Bavaria. It is also a weisse that well illustrates the many seasonal and annual variables that make brewing such a fascinating, and often frustrating, art.

Each spring, Denison's brewer and president, Michael Hancock, eagerly awaits his new shipment of the prince's special German wheat beer yeast so that he might commence with the brewing of the seasonal weisse. This is no ordinary yeast that Hancock has delivered; it is one of the oldest strains in Germany and a wheat yeast with a particular propensity toward the production of banana esters in beer. Not that such flavors are uncommon in German-style wheats — they actually form part of the backbone of the style — but the prince's yeast seems to possess a genuinely cantankerous personality and Denison's weisse has, in some years, been known to carry an almost overwhelming banana character.

THE LEMON QUESTION

Aside from the ubiquitous lime served with a certain Mexican lager, nowhere in the world of beer is citrus used more than with wheat beers. From Halifax to San Diego and Victoria to Miami, whenever a person tries to order a wheat beer, it seems that there is always a waiter or bartender insistently ready to slap a piece of lemon on the side of one's glass. But do we really need lemon with our beer?

The practice of drinking wheat beer with citrus, according to *Michael Jackson's Beer Companion*, did indeed originate in Germany, but no one is exactly sure why. Stories are told, each of which Mr. Jackson disbelieves, but the only fact known for certain is that the tradition goes back many years. When wheat beers were imported to North America, both physically in bottles and kegs and stylistically at our breweries, we unquestioningly adopted the lemon practice, as well.

With the exception of Belgian-style wits, which should never be polluted with lemon, wheat beers are certainly not harmed by the addition of lemon juice. On the other hand, neither may they be especially helped. It all boils down to personal preference and, as with all such matters, there will be advocates aplenty on both sides of the issue. Personally, I don't like the lemon, but my colleague Mr. Jackson writes that he enjoys its effect in a weisse. So, there you have it: two men, two palates and two equally valid opinions.

(Except that I'm right.)

In the summer of 1994, however, Hancock's considerable brewing ability met with just the right temperament of the prince's yeast and a minor classic was born. The banana esters hit the perfect level, the clove flavor balanced beautifully and the weisse proved to be the finest example of its style brewed outside of Germany that I have ever had the honor of tasting. Although not hugely refreshing (a beer of such fruitiness can only be so quenching), that 1994 weisse was a true warm-weather treat. Many times, though not as often as I would have liked, I relinquished myself to its pleasures, most often on a breathtakingly sunny day following a casual Saturday stroll arm-in-arm with my wife. In that context, not even the absence of a patio from the Denison's configuration could detract from the enjoyment of so fine a beer. As seasonal brands do not, and should not, foster absolute consistency, it is hard to say when the weisse will again reach such a pinnacle of taste, but for that one summer, Denison's gorgeous weisse was beer enjoyment itself.

SUNNY SUNDAYS

Summer provides some of the finest moments in North American life, especially in the northern parts where we relish our break from the snow and cold. It is a time to be outdoors, whether playing sports, strolling in the park or relaxing on the terrace or patio and, skin cancer worries notwithstanding, it is a time to worship the sun, relish the warm rain and bask in the silken breezes. Summer gives our spirits wings, allowing us a chance to soar after having been cooped up in our houses, apartments and offices during the more serious winter months.

For some people, myself included, summer reaches its zenith when "those lazy, hazy, crazy days of summer" become more than a song lyric; in other words, when the best summer activity becomes no activity at all. This is also a time when wheat beer shines — though not necessarily the German weisse, but the spicy, refreshing and impossibly quenching Belgian style of white beer.

In a sense, the Belgian wheat style is a perfect partner for the sun. Pour a white beer in the shade and it is just a cloudy, sandy brown beer, but pour it in the sun and it becomes a shining, shimmering testament to the brewer's artistry. Drink one in the dark and it is a light, quirky and palatable quaff, but enjoy a white in the brilliant sunshine and it yields a fruit tree of flavors and a garden of spices. The Belgian wheat and the sun are like the union of a perfectly suited couple; each one makes the other look that much better.

For an idyllic glimpse into the symbiosis that exists between sun and white beer, try the following recipe for a Sunday afternoon. You will need three or four bottles of Belgian-style wheat beer, such as the Celis White or the Blanche de Chambly from Unibroue, and a selection of cheeses, deli meats, perhaps a few radishes or kosher dills and bread. If you already have these ingredients in the house, great. If you don't, pick them up at the market on your way back from the magazine shop.

The reason you will be returning from your local magazine store is that you will need to go there in order to buy about 20 bucks' worth of newspapers and magazines; nothing specific, just whatever you feel like reading that day. If you can, walk or bicycle to the store for your reading material — remember, this is a lazy Sunday summer afternoon. If you have to drive, do so — but wish that you weren't.

When you have your food, magazines and beer, find a quiet corner somewhere outside: a patio, deck or park. (If you have to go to a public location like a park, bring a cooler and an opaque glass so that the authorities won't be able to ruin your pleasure. They wouldn't understand.) Make sure that the place you choose is comfortable and has some shade as well as sun because you're going to be there for a while.

Now you're ready for as pleasurable a Sunday as you will ever experience. Open your first magazine and your first beer, tear off a hunk of bread, slice some cheese and settle back for a hedonistic afternoon of classic, "I don't give a damn and to hell with the world" relaxation. If you have someone you love to share the day with, so much the better, but don't talk too much; just read, eat and steal secretive glances at each other between sips of beer. If it is too hot for you, have some cold water at the ready for drinking or pouring over your head, but don't rush indoors at the first bead of sweat. You will get used to the temperature and besides, you breathe air-conditioned air all week at work, why would you want more of the same on the weekend? Relax, take it easy and take your time; it's summer and there is no need to rush.

When the sun sets or you run out of reading material, gather up your belongings and go inside. Now lie down of your couch or bed, with the fan on high, and have a nap. After all, you deserve it, you've been working hard all day on your mental health.

LAWN-MOWER BEER

You are sitting in your home, expecting no visitors, when the doorbell suddenly rings and you find yourself visited by an old and dear friend whom you see but once a year. Your reaction?

Well, if you are like most North Americans, you would probably roll out the welcome mat, offering up your best food and drink to your honored guest, and this would be a perfectly natural and understandable response because you would be thrilled with the occasion and would want to make the most of it. Yet, when the once-a-year visit from summer rolls around, North Americans tend to react in quite the opposite way. Rather than take advantage of the best the summer's beers have to offer, we pop open can after can of ice-cold, barely flavorful commercial lager, a drink we generally award about the same amount of attention we would a glass of water or lemonade. Even those who consider their beer carefully during the other three seasons tend to retreat to their old habits of drinking mass-production lagers during the summer, justifying their selection by saying that it's just "lawn-mower beer."

But just as one of the secret joys of summer is *not* mowing the lawn, one of the season's gastronomic thrills should be *not* drinking lawn-mower beer. Just because it's summer does not mean that you should have to settle for what is expected.

Certainly among the worthiest of summer brews are those of the pilsner style, including that frequently maligned (by beer connoisseurs, at least) gem, the continental pilsner. While it is true that, at its worst, the continental pilsner is simply a European equivalent of a North American lager, when the style is brewed in the classic manner, it can be an ideal summer quaff. It just has to be put into the proper perspective.

One summer day not too many years ago, I was engaged in a prolonged session of hacky-sack with a group of my mates — hacky-sack being, for the uninitiated, a game that involves the airborne maintenance of a small ball using one's feet only. While admittedly not a tremendously strenuous activity, my colleagues and I were working up a powerful thirst in the hot sun and so we dispatched one of our players to procure a few bottles of cold beer. We had no idea what he would return with.

Our friend returned with Upper Canada Lager, a beer that some might classify as German in style but which I liken to a continental pils as it should be brewed. Although I had more Bohemian thoughts on my mind, I graciously took the beer that was offered and, somewhat to my surprise, found it to be immensely thirst-quenching. The presence of moderate hopping combined with a marginally grainy character, and a perfect temperature, placed this beer at the top of my list for the type of occasion when most people would turn to lawn-mower beer. If you are looking for straight thirst-quenching, I suggest cold water and plenty of it. But, if you desire thirst-quenching with style and body, I recommend a good continental pilsner.

BUFF BREWS

In Gainesville, Florida, there exists a home-brewing club known as the Nude Brewers. Naturists and beer aficionados, this group delights in pursuing their club activities *au naturel* and even once posed for a photo, with coyly placed towels, hands and beer glasses, for the *Southern Draft Brew News*, thus achieving a certain amount of infamy. Though I question the soundness of brewing in the buff, a practice some of the group apparently enjoy, I fully understand their appreciation of the naked pleasures of beer.

Gonzo journalist Hunter S. Thompson has at times described the pleasures of dining on a huge breakfast while perusing several forests' worth of newspapers on his porch in Colorado, naked. An interesting notion, to be sure, but one that is completely unattainable for someone like myself who is not at all inclined toward the consumption of food within two or three hours of waking. Move the setting to an afternoon and add a few bottles of beer, on the other hand, and you have my attention.

Great gastronomy, I have always thought, is best enjoyed unencumbered by the vestments and trappings of society. I have never understood how a man is supposed to fully relish a meal while being strangled by a necktie, nor can I fathom the reasoning behind a woman's donning some equally restrictive outfit for dining out. Eating and drinking are the second and third most natural actions on the planet, the first one being obvious to anyone beyond puberty, and so logic dictates that the ultimate state in which the activities should be pursued would be as naked as the day you were born.

This is not to suggest that I expect to see an explosion of clothing-optional restaurants hit the continent anytime soon — I do not. Rather, I think that the nude enjoyment of food and drink should be tried by everyone at least once in their lives. And what better time to try it than during that scantiest of seasons, summer.

If you have a secluded patio, you can quite easily attain at least a momentary slice of paradise by indulging yourself in a little *al fresco plus* living any fine summer day. Just take a few bottles of your favorite brew — light ales make for particularly fine naked drinking, don't ask me why — and establish your clothingless self in a non-metal chair or chaise lounge out on your porch. You may wish to take along some iced summer fruit, making sure that your beer is of a compatible style, and lazily nosh on it while you enjoy a taste of pure, unrestricted gastronomic sensations. Ah, what luxury!

Anyone living in an unrelentingly urban situation, however, knows that naked patio living is a luxury that is roughly as obtainable as a Rolls-Royce or a 50-foot yacht, and so might feel that such pleasures are beyond their grasp. Well, fear not, Oh city dweller, because such *au naturel* living is not exclusively reserved for a fortunate few. The only difference is that you will have to indulge indoors.

The means are virtually the same: lightly chilled beer, fruit or other nonbread comestibles (those crumbs get *everywhere*!) and pure, unencumbered relaxation. But because you cannot luxuriate outdoors for fear of arrest, you will have to attempt a replication in your own abode. Try putting soft, relaxing music on your stereo, opening all the windows to encourage whatever breeze may be in the air and turn on a fan (preferably a ceiling fan) so that it blows lazily upon yourself. Forget your cares and responsibilities and bask in the pleasures of the moment, the food and the beer. And don't be surprised if everything tastes just a little better than you remember.

Fall

....

THE SEASON'S BOUNTY

It matters not where you live, north or south or east or west, autumn is harvesttime. If you live in the country, you know that it's fall by the carloads of urbanites driving around in search of produce stands, and if you are a city dweller, even one without a car, you know that the season is upon you by the crates of fruits and vegetables that suddenly dominate your local market. Autumn is the time to reap the rich yields of the land, and the brewery.

There are many ways to celebrate the harvest and each family has its own set of autumnal traditions. Some families will, for example, have a final barbecue party of the season and load the grill with corn and hot dogs and bell peppers and hamburgers. Others will participate in the annual ritual of "doing the fall colors" by driving to densely forested areas and reveling in the multihued wonders of nature. Still others will rush to the beach for that one last, glorious corn roast. But regardless of what your personal tradition might be, a little beer is sure to add to the celebration.

While it is not unheard of for breweries to release new beers in the fall, it is most often the case that all the new brands will have been released well before the end of the prime summer season or held back for winter festivities. As such, the beers of the fall are most often the same beers you have been enjoying throughout the spring and summer, with one stylistic exception: the Oktoberfest märzen.

OCTOBER'S FESTIVAL

Even most non-beer drinkers are familiar with Munich's famous Oktoberfest and the traditions that it brings with it. It is therefore hardly surprising that numerous homespun versions of the fall festival take place throughout North America each year, including the Kitchener-Waterloo Oktoberfest in Ontario, the largest such celebration held outside of the Munich fest. These events range from one-day affairs held at the local brewery or bar to megadollar extravaganzas that draw thousands of tourists, generate millions of dollars' worth of economic impact and threaten at times to engulf their host city. North Americans have embraced the annual Oktoberfest with a passion.

Unfortunately, the breweries and beer drinkers of this continent have not taken to the traditional beer style of Oktoberfest with quite the enthusiasm that they have shown for the festival itself. For all of the Oktoberfests to be found around the land, there is still precious little märzen being brewed in North America's microbreweries.

This paucity of märzen is a shame, too, because it is the ideal beer style for the season and is especially appropriate for Oktoberfest celebrations. A märzen's Vienna lager qualities make it a beautifully versatile beer, as comfortable beside a plate of sausage and sauerkraut as it is next to smoked pork and potato salad, and its bottom-fermented origins allow it to have a modestly refreshing quality, even at its warmingly elevated alcohol content of 5–6.5% by volume. Certainly these are ideal characteristics for a beer to be enjoyed in the variable weather of autumn at a festival where good food and good beer can reasonably be expected to dominate.

Because as much as Oktoberfesting is about beer, it is equally about food, music and merriment. There can be nothing festival-like about hundreds of people sitting around in silence in a big tent while drinking beer. There must be mountains of succulent food, a band or two and an overpowering air of joviality permeating the entire festival area, even if that area happens to be the whole town! At the best of Oktoberfests, these elements will assume a status at least equal to that of the beer, although the brews will continue to grab the headlines and photo ops.

My favorite vision of a perfect Oktoberfest involves a long table filled end-to-end with friends and acquaintances, some of whom I have even known for longer than five minutes. The weather is crisp in that typically autumn way, but the sun is shining bright and the nip in the air calls for only a light jacket. As the band plays the sort of raucous oompah-pah music that most North Americans can only tolerate at a German-style beer hall, the table is piled high with steaming sausages, golden cutlets, heaping bowls of sauerkraut side by side with potato salad and pots of sweetly hot mustard scattered here and there. And then the beer arrives, pitchers of medium gold or reddish-brown märzen from Stoudt (Fest), Catamount (Oktoberfest) and Brasal (Spécial). What a fall festival feast!

MORE FALL FEASTS

Oktoberfest is not the only place to celebrate the harvest season or, for that matter, is it necessarily the best. For autumn means much more gastronomically than the traditional but limited food selection of that October rite. And when it comes to celebrating the fall, the key word is *plenty*.

Although I am an unrepentant meat eater, the fall is the only season in which I feel that I could easily turn to vegetarianism. There is simply so much fresh produce in our markets and grocery stores during that time of the year that it is virtually impossible to ignore how spectacularly flavorful everything looks. Oh sure, it is true that in these days of high-speed transport and scientific farming techniques, we can get fruits and vegetables of all sorts all year round, but none of those out-of-season foodstuffs ever seem to come close to honest, local produce picked fresh off the vine, tree or stalk, or pulled from the earth, not more than a few days earlier.

In southern Ontario each fall, a charitable event called the Feast of Fields is held in which top chefs from around the region prepare some of their finest dishes and serve them, along with local wines and beers, smack-dab in the middle of the fields of a regional farm or vineyard. When the weather cooperates, the effect of partaking of such magnificent food and drink so near to the earth that spawned it is positively life-affirming. It is no wonder that the event is consistently sold out, even when the weather is less than perfect.

In the same vein, if on a decidedly smaller scale, I am reminded of the cornfield parties I used to have with my friends when I was in my teens. On such occasions, we would drive out to the nearest farmland on a warm autumn night and locate an adequately obscure side road that ran by a cornfield. After finding a spot for the car, we would trudge into the field and greedily avail ourselves of all the corn we could possibly consume, and a bit more. Our next stop would be a clearing where we could build a small fire and roast our ill-gotten goods until they could be gluttonously devoured, no butter or salt required. Looking back, I feel badly for those poor farmers in whose fields we effected our raids, but the memory of how delicious that corn tasted eases the guilt considerably.

Of course, responsible adults do not go around breaking the law by stealing corn in the middle of the night. Far better that we should save our illegalities for when the enjoyment of a fine brew in the great outdoors is not only called for but insisted upon by the glories of the fall season.

Outdoor fall feasting first requires that you take a trip to the country and find an isolated clearing far away from any signs of urban life. Ideally, your chosen spot should be on a hillside overlooking a forested glen where the leaves of the trees are in their colorful death throes, but this is not a necessity if no such area is available. Far better that you sacrifice the reds, oranges and rusts of the foliage in favor of a totally uninhabited site, if the two characteristics are indeed mutually exclusive.

Unlike the quiet, reflective qualities of summer that beget solitude and introspection, the fall requires people, as many as possible, for its proper observance. If you can fill your car with eager outdoor eaters, do so, and if you can find two or three carloads of folks to bring along, so much the better. As long as everyone is well behaved, there is no reason that this cannot become a small party.

A PINT AND A BED

One old European brewing tradition that is catching on in North America, albeit very slowly, is the idea of the brewery–inn, a place where food, beer and lodging are accorded equal respect. Two such establishments are the Norwich Inn in Norwich, Vermont, and the Swans Hotel in Victoria, British Columbia. Three time zones apart, they form the perfect bookends for the North American brewery–inn movement.

Fast approaching its bicentennial anniversary, the Norwich Inn is a charming and historic guest house situated on the Vermont–New Hampshire border. It is distinguished by 15 elegantly rustic rooms in the main house, with another seven available in the Carriage House, and its many touches of old New England charm. It is also home to what at the time of writing was likely the smallest commercial brewery in North America.

Sally Wilson already owned and operated the inn when she met and fell in love with her now–husband Tim. An avid homebrewer, Tim persuaded Sally to forfeit the couple's own kitchen to turn it into a brewery for the Norwich Inn in 1993. Working with a brewhouse that consisted of gas-fired kettles made out of converted beer kegs, Tim has been producing impressive ales at the rate of about 70–80 barrels per year ever since. When I last visited him in the fall of 1994, he told me that he intended to construct a larger brewery with a 500-barrel annual capacity on site sometime during 1995. Regardless of the scale, however, as long as Tim keeps turning out sumptuous brews like his Stackpole Porter, I certainly know where I'll be staying in Vermont.

The Swans opened in 1989 as a luxurious suites-only hotel with an expansive bar area and what must rank as among the largest pub-based breweries I have ever come across. Located in the heart of Victoria, the brewpub does a booming business every night of the week and hotel vacancies are increasingly rare. It is a happy situation for owner Michael Williams, and one that is hardly surprising when you note the abundant charms effected throughout the building.

Each of the 29 distinctive suites in the Swans is an exercise in aesthetics, with Michael providing his own impressive collection of Canadian art — one of the most comprehensive such private collections in the country — as a sort of revolving decor. Chris Johnson is the Swans's young brewer and he is quickly coming into his own in the brewery, producing six types of ale, lager and stout as well as rotating specialties. Upon my last visit, he offered me a taste of what I thought to be his finest brew yet, a deliciously malty Scotch ale. And when you can get a pint of such tasty ale delivered to the door of your suite by room service, it certainly adds considerably to the enjoyment of one's stay.

If you are a city dweller, you will likely find it beneficial to leave for your trip with no food at all in your picnic basket. You are, after all, headed to where the great produce of the season has been grown, so why bother paying inflated city prices for your goods? Far better to pick them up en route and let availability dictate what you will be enjoying. Pack the cooler, though, because it is unlikely that you will find the kind of beer selection in the country that you have access to in the city. Pick a couple of weizens, a märzen or three, perhaps a bock, a pair of brown ales and a few fruit-flavored brews, along with a light ale and several nonalcoholic drinks for your poor driver. And, of course, multiply those numbers if you have a gang larger than five or so.

You will need to bring along such items as knives, plastic plates, unbreakable glassware and a couple of blankets. Leave the hibachi and charcoal at home; you don't need meat at this feast and, even if you feel that you do, one of those deliciously greasy salamis with skins as tough as leather will do beautifully. A Frisbee, baseball, football or other recreational equipment is purely optional and, in fact, discouraged. There should be enough joy in the food, drink and company to keep you plenty occupied without the need of things flying through the air at decapitating levels and speeds.

As for the food, aside from what you will buy directly from the farmers, all you should need are a few loaves of fresh bread and some aged cheeses. Put that together with juicy, red tomatoes still warm from the vine, fresh cucumbers with paper-thin skins, ivory white radishes, tender and crisp bell peppers in all the colors of the rainbow — except green, you can get those anytime — and some scallions or other sweet, young onions. You may also wish to add some of the pickles or olives prepared by the proprietor of the local country store and, for sweets, pick up a basket of fresh peaches or grapes, or one of each. When you find your clearing, spread out all the food on a blanket and invite everyone to enjoy as much as they want. And celebrate the season the way it was meant to be celebrated.

THE FRUITS OF THEIR LABORS

Another way I enjoy marking the fall is by sampling the best of the growing range of fruit beers on the market these days. True, such brands may be for sale on a year-round basis and their connection to the fall might be marginal at best, but it still somehow feels right.

The traditional fruits of the beer world are the cherries and raspberries that Belgian brewers have been putting into their lambics for centuries. In North America, however, fruit additions from apricots to chili peppers, and blueberries to passion fruit, are fast becoming almost commonplace and it now seems that there is nothing some experimental brewer will not be willing to toss into a brew. And while traditionalists may fight this odd, fruity trend, I say it is better to just go with the flow and reap the ofttimes delicious benefits.

The best time of the day to taste fruit beers is early afternoon, when the sun is shining brightly enough to vividly illuminate the brilliant colors of the beers. Often, although not always, these flavored brews will reflect the hues of their ingredient fruits in subtle ways and natural light provides the best medium by which to appreciate their tones. Like any tasting, a fruit beer sampling is also best accomplished in the company of friends, so a Saturday or Sunday afternoon might work best.

Because of the wide variety of fruit you may be showcasing, it is an especially good idea when tasting flavored brews to do so in an environment as free as possible of all other aromas. Moreover, despite the often logical temptation to serve them at refrigerator temperature, these beers will best release their bouquets and the full range of their flavors when they are presented at cellar temperature.

Try to accumulate a diversity of fruit flavors for your tasting, including anything from Buffalo Bill's famous Pumpkin Ale to the extraordinarily balanced Pyramid Apricot Ale. You may also want to run the gamut on the intensity of flavors offered, from the tangy and undeniably raspberry-ish Sangre de Frambuesa of Santa Fe Brewing to the more subtle fruitiness of the famed fruit beers of Marin Brewing. Variety is not only the spice of life, it is the heart of your tasting.

Since most people are still relatively unfamiliar with the wide range of available fruit beers, the simple presentation of a diverse group of such brews should be enough to impress even the most critical of your guest tasters. If you really want to end with a flourish, however, you may wish to put aside a bowl filled with samples of all those fruits you tried in the beers and bring it out along with some other food when the initial sampling has finished and the pure enjoyment begins.

The beauty of fruit beer tastings as opposed to other style grouping is that these beers come in such a huge assortment of types, flavors and intensities. No one can proceed with their sampling in an incorrect order because who is to say that a cherry beer should be tasted after a blueberry beer yet before a peach beer? There can be no pressures, perceived or otherwise, in a fruit beer tasting, just a love of fruit, a fascination with the creation of a specialty beer by a skilled brewer and, of course, a celebration of harvesttime.

Winter

....

FIRESIDE BREWS

The season of Santa Claus, skis and snowmen is not generally thought of as a prime time for beer appreciation in North America. No doubt this state of affairs has much to do with our continental obsession with serving beer at ice-cold temperatures — who needs a frigid brew when the outside temperature is dipping well into the minuses? — and the lack of body offered by the dominant beer brands. But, just like everything else having to do with beer on this continent, this attitude is slowly changing.

Many beer styles fit quite nicely with the northern winter climates of such states as New York and Montana and most of the Canadian provinces. These brews are generally of higher strength, bigger body and more forceful personality than others and are not the sort that require significant refrigeration. They are the beers of fireside contemplation, candle-lit conversation and cuddling with a loved one; they are the winter warmers.

The term "winter warmer" is a somewhat ambiguous one. Originally used to describe strong and usually sweet English ales, it is often used today as a catchall for any beer that happens to be of above-average alcohol level and fairly rich and thick in its body. My inclination is toward the latter categorization, although this is a strictly personal peccadillo and I have no solid argument to back it up. Then again, with beers as lovely as many of the best winter warmers, who has need of arguing?

Taking the broader approach to winter warmer classification, I can include a fair range in the category: Scotch ales, strong ales, imperial stouts, some Belgian-style ales, doppelbocks, eisbocks and barley wines. The only test that need be passed to gain admittance to this none-too-exclusive club of brews is what I call my Fireside Exam.

One of the oddities of the apartment in which I live with my wife is that it has a fireplace in the kitchen. Now, while this may be a perfectly normal situation for a country cottage or a hundred-year-old estate house, it is certainly a curiosity in a second-floor flat just outside the heart of downtown Toronto and we thought as much when we moved into the place. It has, however, turned out to be a huge benefit in many ways, one of which is the implementation of the fireside winter warmer test.

The way the test works is this: In the heart of winter, my wife and I light a fire and sit down to enjoy a lengthy, leisurely dinner with the fireplace to one side of our table and several candles of varying sizes and shapes to the other. These meals can range from one to three courses but will always take about two hours or so to complete, and all this in advance of the test. When dinner has ended, we pull our chairs up close to the fire and relax and digest, she usually with a glass of port and I with a snifter of strong, malty beer. If the beer in my hand fits with the motif of the night, if it just *feels right*, and it warms the body and stimulates the soul, then it qualifies as a winter warmer.

The beauty of this test is that it can be conducted by anyone with access to good food and a fireplace — in a pinch, extra candle power can be substituted for the fireplace — and it requires no deep thought or excessive taste analysis. The only other thing you need is a willingness to relax.

APRÈS SKI

For many aficionados of the sport, from competitive athletes to "ski bunnies," no winter activity beats a day spent on the slopes. Cold weather, cloud cover, long lift lineups and mediocre conditions offer no discouragement for these dedicated individuals, skiing is their joy and the ski hill their home away from home. Yet as devoted as any ski enthusiast may be, no one can spend all day, every day on the hill. Eventually, it comes time to return to the lodge at the base of the mountain and partake of the pleasures of what is commonly known as après ski.

When I was a skier, I always enjoyed the après part more than the actual skiing itself and, back then, I was not even of drinking age. The camaraderie of the lodge appealed to me, as did the warmth of the ever-present fireplace or stove and the cozy, rustic setting. I may not have been much of a skier, but I was *great* at après ski!

Fortunately, you need not be a skier or, for that matter, anywhere near a ski run in order to enjoy the après ski spirit. Cold weather, a sprinkling of snow on the ground (or a cold, cruel rain for you southerners) and a friendly pub are all you need for a full appreciation of the post-skiing ideal, plus, of course, a good beer.

Any of the above-mentioned winter warmer styles will suffice for the enjoyment of the ski lodge feeling but, for that ultimate "just off the slopes" believability, I recommend something that would not feel out of place in a snifter or tulip-shaped beer glass, a brew high in strength yet not especially heavy on the sweetness. In short, a barley wine.

The barley wine style beer, as most are officially known, has grown tremendously in popularity over the past few years and has now become something of a staple style in many brewpubs. The classic North American barley wines remain, as ever, Anchor Old Foghorn, Sierra Nevada Bigfoot and Rogue Old Crustacean, with the Rogue being the least senior of the three. Each of these beers is strong, fairly dry, notoriously complex and positively delicious, especially when sipped at hearthside in the arms of your mate.

With qualities such as these, it is no wonder that barley wines are the ideal elixir for that après ski sensation, whether earned through hours of shushing on the slopes or simply fabricated for its sheer, luxurious pleasures. Pour some into a brandy snifter, grab the most comfortable, cushiest seat by the fire and let yourself sink into the tender, exquisite grasp of both cushion and barley wine.

And then brag to your friends about that dangerous mogul you negotiated, even if it was traversed only in your mind.

CHRISTMAS BEERS

It is something that you can rely upon to return every year like clockwork, resurrected like Lazarus and bringing with it the exact same trappings year after year after year. No, I am not referring to Christmas — *that* I love — rather, the subject matter under discussion here is the endless debate over the *commercialization* of Christmas.

The arguments for both sides have been presented relentlessly, especially over the last decade or so, with no end in sight. And at each and every Christmas season, it seems like the Season's Greetings banners, plastic elves, red-clad salespeople and artificially snowy glitz comes out earlier and earlier. Every manufacturer, distributor, storekeeper and service person is getting into the act, and now you expect me to tell you that North America's microbreweries are following suit, right?

Wrong.

True, breweries are coming out with seasonal winter and Christmas beers at warp speed these days, but such delights are a long way from the crass commercialization of your neighborhood department store. Far from cashing in on the season, the microbrewed beers of Christmas are designed to glorify and exalt its spirit. Truly, they are celebration brews. Certainly among the earliest Christmas beers to appear on the market was Anchor Brewing's Our Special Ale, a beer that is brewed differently every year and is made only in small batches, never released before American Thanksgiving and seldom available for long after. Incredibly, Anchor's Christmas seasonal was first brewed in 1975, quite some time before the microbrewing industry took off on this continent, and it has enjoyed near-legendary status among beer lovers ever since. In the true tenor of the season, Fritz Maytag, the man who resurrected Anchor in 1965 and is generally considered the father of American craft brewing, says that he wants Our Special Ale to be his brewery's gift to his customers, and a unique and exciting gift at that.

THE BEST JOKE OF ALL

One of my fondest beer-related memories concerns not a particular beer find or taste but a practical joke my friends and I pulled on one of our housemates during my university days. I think it demonstrates beautifully the passion people have toward their beer.

The time period was back in the lean-and-mean era of beer drinking in Ontario, when the microbrewery renaissance was still in its infancy, exciting imports were few and far between and commercial brands from the big breweries dominated the beer market to the exclusion of all else. It was New Year's Day and one of my eight or so housemates, Scott, was off to meet his parents for dinner, leaving the rest of us to our own devices. Upon his departure, Scott left us specific instructions not to drink any of his almost-full case of Brick Lager, and *particularly not his coveted six-pack of Kronenbourg.*

Of course, a long family meal is more than enough time for mischievous minds to conjure up a good joke and, besides, we needed something with which to occupy ourselves for the evening. So we set to work devising a simple, yet brilliantly funny, plan.

The first step was to hide all of Scott's beer save for one bottle of Kronenbourg, which we left in the six-pack case in the refrigerator; somehow that seemed crueler than simply hiding all of it. Next, we proceeded to the basement where empty bottles were kept until they could be returned for deposit and pulled up 24 empties of the same brand that Scott had ordered us not to drink. We scattered these bottles around the living room and sat back to await our prey's return.

When he returned from his meal a couple of hours later, Scott was incensed from the moment he entered the living room. Not only did it appear that we had drunk his beer against his expressed wishes, but from the looks of the room, poor Scott could only conclude that we had drunk it all! He called us every name in the book, at steadily increasing volume.

The decibel level went up several notches as Scott found that his imported brew had also been consumed and he was even more furious (if that were possible) as he reentered the living room, off-balanced six-pack case in hand, to scream at us some more.

The sheer and absolute beauty of the gag finally got to be too much as first one, and then all of us broke into laughter at Scott's expense. He quickly caught on and, after we had shown him his cache of beer, we all shared a few and had a good chuckle. I don't think that Scott has ever quite forgiven us, though.

Today, the Christmas season brings with it a host of specially brewed beers sold exclusively around the holidays, and, following the Anchor example, many of them change in taste annually. There are Vancouver Island Brewing's treacly Hermannator doppelbock, Rhino Chasers medium-bodied Winterful, Sierra Nevada Brewing's intensely hoppy Celebration Ale and Rogue's even hoppier Mogul Ale, Portland Brewing's complexly floral Icicle Creek Winter Ale, the relatively dry Samuel Adams Winter Lager, the Brooklyn Brewery's remarkably rich Black Chocolate Stout, Redhook's superbly balanced Winterhook, the milk chocolaty Festive Brown Ale from Ontario's Hart Breweries and the raspberry- and nutmeg-flavored Pete's Wicked Winter Brew. And that's just the tip of the iceberg, or the Christmas tree!

As befits beers designed with the holidays in mind, these Christmas brews and, indeed, virtually all Christmas beers are best enjoyed in the company of family or close friends. There is something very intimate about sharing such special beers; the feeling of well-being they produce when sampled among kith and kin is second to few other beer-tasting experiences.

When I return to the home of my parents around Christmastime each year, I always make an attempt to bring along a sampling of different brews for everyone to enjoy. In the winter of 1994, that selection included several bottles of different Christmas beers I had left over from a tasting I had conducted for the *Southern Draft Brew News*.

I had no idea whether or not these beers would be warmly received; neither did I know whether I and my wife might end up being the only ones doing the tasting. Nonetheless, upon arrival I cheerily pulled the beers out of our luggage only to find that I was actually adding to the set of sample brews my sister and her husband had brought with them from out West. It was truly shaping up to be a grand Christmas beer sampling.

The tasting, about as informal as they come, took place in my parents' kitchen with all of us standing around the open bottles and swapping opinions on the different brews. The hoppiness of the Sierra Nevada Celebration Ale was much discussed, as was the comparative subtlety of the Granville Island 10th Anniversary Ale, and the Redhook Winterhook proved to be especially popular with my father. There was sharing, offering, giving and enjoyment aplenty in the kitchen that day; all of the ingredients of the true Christmas spirit.

CHAPTER 5

A BEER AT THE TABLE

Beer really is a remarkable drink.

Think about it; beer can refresh and quench or fulfill and satisfy; it is undeniably a beverage, yet it has nutritive qualities more in keeping with a foodstuff; it comes in colors ranging from pale yellow to jet black, and just about every shade in between, and offers flavors from fruit and nuts to mocha and licorice; and it is as at home at a barbecue or ball game as it is at a society event or theater intermission. Name one other drink that can do all that!

And yet, these credentials notwithstanding, North Americans still tend to sell beer short when it comes to the single most revered and socially important site in any house: the dining-room table. There, wine is king and coffee and tea may play supporting roles, with liqueurs or brandies as bit players, but beer is banished. It may make it as far as predinner cocktails, but, please, leave your beer at the dining-room door.

Beer gets no spot at the table partly as a result of the bad PR that has dogged the beverage over the years and partly because of a lack of understanding. Yet beer actually has a wonderful ability to marry with all sorts of food; the misconceptions about beer's relation to food should be cleared up forthwith and the negative press it has received must be preempted by understanding. Beer's place at the table should be secured and its abilities recognized; to do otherwise is to risk leaving our first-round draft pick on the bench while we play the game with fourth-stringers. (And, yes, the pun was intended.)

DINING WITH BEER

When taking beer into your dining room for the first time, it is quite natural to be a little hesitant. After all, your guests are likely expecting wine, and where a mismatched wine served with the main course will be over-looked when the food is plentiful and the conversation lively, a beer served with your meal will fall under much closer scrutiny. This will happen not because your guests are snobs, but because the mere act of serving beer instead of wine, and thus thumbing your nose at convention, will draw attention to what you have done. Your food and beer pairings will be evaluated simply because you have selected beer instead of wine.

But who cares!

Wine snobs may trumpet the "sophistication" of fermented grape juice relative to the alchemic magic of beer, but the fact is that beer is far more versatile in its role at the table than is wine. How many wines marry well with chocolate, for example? Or chicken vindaloo? Or raw onions? Beer can meet all of these challenges, and many more.

As with all things gastronomic, success in pairing beer and food is largely dependent on experience. There will be times when you just have to use your instincts in deciding which beer to serve with a dish and it certainly helps to have had those instincts honed through practice. Attending beer dinners where the matches have been made by skilled chefs and veteran beverage managers or guest hosts from the beer industry is one way to garner some valuable experience. Another, perhaps less expensive, way is to practice with your daily meals at home.

It is a given that if you wish to work on your beer and food instincts, you will have to have a range of beer styles available in your refrigerator or cellar. Fortunately, stocking a variety of beer will not cost so much as, say, establishing an extensive wine cellar. A few bottles of one or two good examples of ten or 12 styles will certainly suffice, and if this selection is gathered over the course of several weeks, the financial toll will hardly be noticeable.

Once you have assembled your beer cellar, it will be time to start playing with various tastes. Now, while this may be starting to sound like a classroom exercise, I can assure you that the word *playing* was chosen for a very specific reason: this is fun! Finding beer brands and styles that perfectly complement even the most unlikely foods gives rise to a whole new dimension of beer enjoyment. Whether it is as simple a food as a chocolate chip cookie or as complex a taste as a Cajun gumbo, discovering the exact beer to set it off is an achievement akin to solving a particularly difficult crossword puzzle, and at least as satisfying.

But there is no need to enter blindly into your beer- and food-mating adventures. There are several rules of thumb to lead you on your way, as well as many specific guidelines that pertain to individual foods. For now, though, let's concentrate on the generalities.

RED AND WHITE = ALE AND LAGER?

Sometime, somewhere, someone in history decided that red wine was to be served with red meats and white wine with white meats. As a dining rule, it was okay for starters, but quickly wore out its welcome as the gastronome discovered the intricacies of wine and the variety of full- and light-bodied wines residing under both color banners. The equation also neglected to account for rosés, *vins mousseaux*, sherries, ports, madeiras and other products of the grape, and made no allowances for cooking styles and spicing.

I mention this antiquated wine rule only because there is a similar canon for beer: ale with red meat and lager for white or, more broadly, treat ales as you would red wines and lagers as you would white wines. It is a generalization that does work more frequently than not but, like the wine rule, it is fraught with loopholes.

On the positive side of things, ale often does behave as red wine in relation to dining. If, for instance, you had a rare-to-medium roast beef and were contemplating a Côtes du Rhône as an accompaniment, you would not go far wrong in substituting a good ale such as full-bodied brown or a malty Scottish ale. Similarly, a hamburger would do well beside a pint of bitter, and an appetizer of beef carpaccio (marinated and thinly sliced raw beef) would taste splendid when served with a glass of delicate, British-style pale ale.

Likewise, lager will frequently fill the role of a white wine in a most distinguished fashion. Roast chicken? How about a statuesque glass filled with Bohemian-style pilsner in place of a chablis? For a grilled whitefish, a pilsner of any style will likely marry as well as any white wine and grilled pork chops will certainly be well served by a märzen or perhaps its milder cousin, the Vienna lager.

The limits of this relationship are, however, quite severe. The use of the red-white, ale-lager rule would never result in dozens of delightful pairings, such as smoked salmon and stout — a truly memorable seafood-and-beer match — or Vienna lager and Hungarian goulash, to name but two. And where the categories of white and red do encompass most wines, the ale and lager classes ignore whole families of beers such as wheats, bocks and porters. It is obvious, then, that we need other general rules to accompany this one and, fortuitously, such complementary guidelines do exist.

One such general rule, again related to wine, is to treat hoppiness in beer in the same fashion as you would acidity in wine. In other words, where you would use the high acidity of, say, an Alsatian wine to make a wine and food marriage, you can use a hoppy pale ale or German-style pils in its place, often with much more favorable results.

For an example of how this works, you need look no farther than the salted pretzels or peanuts left out on the bar at your local pub. Try eating

THE NOSE KNOWS

In pairing food with beer, or any beverage, it is vitally important to remember the role of aroma in determining flavor. The famous nineteenth-century French gastronome Brillat-Savarin perhaps put it best, or most colorfully, when he noted that "smell and taste form a single sense, of which the mouth is the laboratory and the nose is the chimney; or, to speak more exactly, of which one serves for the tasting of actual bodies and the other for the savoring of their gases."

What Brillat-Savarin was getting at was the fact that the mouth and the nose share the same air passage and so contribute proportionately to the sense we describe as taste. Even if we are not always aware of it, we smell as we taste and, to a lesser degree, taste what we smell. This is why ex-smokers often speak of developing a keener sense of taste after they quit and their olfactory nerve cells begin to regenerate.

It follows, therefore, that aroma will be a factor when deciding which beer to match to any given food. If the beer has an acrid aroma, it is unlikely that it will match well with an overly sweet-smelling food, and similarly, the odds will be against a floral-scented beer standing up to a pungent dish. Of course, there will always be exceptions—forceful bittering hops will sometimes travel incognito, disguised by particularly aromatic hops—but, in general, aroma is a good place to start when arranging marriages between beer and food.

medium-strength Scottish ale or perhaps a porter, in order to match the satisfying "comfort food" qualities of such soups. If the flavor of the soup is fuller and richer still, such as an oxtail or French onion soup, step up the body of your beer to a Scotch or old ale, or even a Belgian-style abbey ale.

One beer quality to avoid in making most cream-free soup pairings is excessive hoppiness. This is because most such soups have a tendency toward sweet or savory characters, two qualities that do not readily welcome bitterness to their sides. For a spicy mulligatawny soup, you might like a pale ale of some sort, and with a Chinese hot and sour soup, a continental pilsner would perform nicely, but those are the exceptions rather than the rules.

A minestrone will welcome a Vienna lager (see The Tomato Issue later in this chapter) and good old cream of tomato will do likewise, although the latter is, in my opinion, best enjoyed with a glass of milk. Beef vegetable screams for a brown ale to match its beefy sweetness, and cold vichyssoise is a delight with a similarly cold white beer to play off the faintly tangy qualities of the leek. Finally, a fish soup such as a lobster bisque or a fish chowder will pair magnificently with a kölsch to match the soft and delicate fish flavor with a delicacy all its own and just a note or two of hop to cut through the cream.

Salad is another dish that assumes many forms on the dining-room table, but here, too, certain types of salad naturally beget certain styles of beer.

For a basic green salad with an oil and vinegar dressing, try a slightly hoppy brown ale to lend a nuttiness to the greens while meeting the acid and oil of the dressing with a soft bitterness. If a creamy dressing has been employed, especially if it has been used liberally, switch to a hoppier and drier pale ale or a crisp pilsner, more likely the latter. If you want to add a real twist to your salad, forgo the beer in the glass and try mixing it right into the salad as a dressing. A tart raspberry beer, with a little malt or red wine vinegar added for pep, can form the base of a very interesting dressing.

Fruit salads or green salads with fruit added pose a tricky dilemma. There will be plenty of acidity from the citrus but, as mentioned above, hops do not tend to perform terribly well with such fruits. On the other hand, a malty beer like a brown ale or märzen will never stand up to the tanginess of the salad. The answer is contained in wheat: a weizen or hefeweizen or, in the case of salads where the fruit does not play a dominant role, a white beer. These wheat-based brews all have a certain acidity to them, even a citric flavor in some cases, and so will be able to meet the fruit salad challenge quite admirably.

RED MEATS

North Americans eat more red meat per capita than any other people in the world. Unfortunately for our gastronomic image, much of this is served up as burgers in fast-food establishments, where it is either illegal to sell beer or the selection is limited to the major brewery brands. Either way, the "dining experience" in these fast-food factories is unlikely to be memorable.

Far more worthy of consideration, however, is the picture of a medium-rare roast beef served at the dining-room table on a Saturday or Sunday evening, with the entire family present and no one in a hurry to rush off to someplace else. This is where a bottle of cabernet or Bordeaux will normally be uncorked for the older, and perhaps younger, family members, but where a fine ale will serve equally well. A rich, British-style pale ale would be a marvelous way to match the strong flavors of the medium-rare

FAT-FREE & CALORIE-WISE

While on the subject of food, it makes sense to visit the realm of what is perhaps the greatest piece of mythology surrounding beer: calories. As a professional beer writer, I am frequently asked how a man in my line of work keeps from putting on the pounds. It is a question that I must admit I find a trifle insulting, because it is based on the assumption that I guzzle a lot of beer in my day-to-day life. The truth is, I probably do drink more beer on a daily basis than most people, but I also remain active and, besides, who says that beer is fattening?

The popular conception, buoyed by media images of beer-drinkin' good ol' boys with bloated beer bellies, is that beer is a fattening beverage. As is often the case with images, however, the truth is quite the opposite. Beer actually has a reasonable number of calories, along with numerous vitamins and carbohydrates, and it is only excessive consumption that leads to obesity. To illustrate this, consider the following numbers from Health and Welfare Canada:

341 mL of 5% alcohol by volume lager = 150 calories
341 mL of 2% fat milk = 176 calories
341 mL of apple juice = 177 calories
341 mL of orange juice (from concentrate) = 173 calories
8 oz (250 mL) rum and coke (2 oz/50 mL rum) = 194 calories

"Well, sure," you say. "That's fine for lagers, but what about heavier beers like stouts and porters?" Surprise! Because most of beer's calories come from alcohol and many dry stouts are actually lighter in that respect than most commercial-strength lagers, stout may even have fewer calories than lager or ale! And, in this age of fat awareness, it should also be noted that beer is and always has been fat-free.

---

beef, with a Scottish ale more appropriate when gravy is offered and a hoppier pale better for more well-done meat.

Another common way to eat beef is in a robust stew and, here, we should take our beer-pairing cues from the Belgians. For although it is not really a stew in the way we normally view such dishes, carbonnade of beef is undoubtedly the ultimate in stove-top beef cookery and so, the grand-daddy of all beef stews. The Belgians will match their carbonnade with a Flemish brown ale, and the pairing of the tender beef and the sweet ale makes for a stunningly delicious meal. Unfortunately for North Americans, this beer style is not brewed on this continent, although it is imported.

Anyways, it might fall slightly short of body for a rich and heavy stew laden with vegetables and soaked in slow-cooked gravy. No, better a robust brown or Scottish ale when the subject is a rib-sticking stew.

Other ways to serve beef will likewise call for medium- to full-bodied ales with mild to moderate amounts of hoppiness: British pale ale for a steak and kidney pie; amber ale or alt for a real hamburger — as opposed to a fast-food one — or a grilled steak; a bitter or a rousse for a tourtière; and a Canadian or cream ale for beef teriyaki.

When preparing lamb or game meats, the call should go out for a very robust and at least somewhat fruity beer to match. This is because such meats have a sweetness to their gaminess and will present a more full and intense flavor than will beef. The range of partner beers, then, will venture from British pale ales to Scotch ales.

For a perfectly roasted leg of lamb, search for a robust Scottish ale to match the heavy flavor of the dish. If a good amount of rosemary and garlic have been used in its preparation, however, something medium-dry with a slightly-more-than-moderate hoppiness would be better suited to the challenge of three rather strong and quite different flavors in union — say, a British pale ale or even a relatively mild IPA.

Buffalo, which is becoming a quite fashionable meat in certain areas, can generally be treated much the same as beef when a marriage with beer is proposed. Be mindful, however, of the need for slightly bolder ales to match the stronger taste of the bison. Fortunately, this will not pose a problem as the buffalo should be leaner than the beef and will therefore not have as much need for some hoppiness to balance the fat.

Venison that you buy at a specialty market or restaurant these days will little resemble what Uncle Earl used to bring home strapped to the hood of his pickup. Commercial meat, being farm-raised, will have a much lighter flavor and lack the heavy gaminess that permeated Uncle Earl's deer. This being the case, a lighter ale that possesses some fruitiness, such as a mild brown ale or a light amber, will serve very nicely.

POULTRY AND PORK

Given the general rule of ale with red meat and lager with white meat, it comes as no surprise that bottom-fermentation will dominate this section in much the same manner as the top-fermented ales ruled the red meat category. And just as red wine will cross the color divide to match well with pork, so will ale infringe on lager's territory where that meat is concerned.

A sweet and fairly delicate meat when cooked and served on its own, chicken has a marvelous ability to adapt to its culinary surroundings, becoming fiery hot as chicken wings or seductively succulent as chicken cordon bleu. Hence, what the bird is cooked with will influence dramatically which beer would best suit it. As a roast, however, or baked or broiled in breasts or legs, chicken's tender character is best paired with a moderately malty lager such as a Vienna or a roasty dunkel.

Something like a chicken kiev, on the other hand, needs a hoppier lager to match the garlic and parsley butter, so a Bohemian pilsner would do quite nicely. In the case of chicken paprika or hot and spicy wings, a cold German pils or a chilled, light pale ale will rule the day with its hop balancing the heat. For chicken cordon bleu, you could go two ways: a märzen to complement the flavor of the cheese or a continental lager to provide a drier counterpoint to the richness of the dish.

If the Christmas goose or a duck is on the table instead of its smaller cousin, you will have to remember to treat the bitterness of the beer as you would the acidity of a good wine and select a brew with a moderate to full hoppiness in order to counter the greasiness of such a bird. Remembering also that these fowl have a significantly stronger flavor than chicken, it is possible to marry them to an ale rather than limiting yourself to a lager. Something like a bitter or a British pale ale will sit beautifully beside one of the bigger birds, and even a hoppy pale bock would not be out of place.

For pork, especially roast pork, märzen makes for a match made in heaven. This applies equally if the meat is done up in sausages or served in chops, but requires some modification if ribs are the cut of the day. Because pork ribs are generally served with either a barbecue sauce or a honey-garlic glaze, they call for a drier beer to balance these strong flavors, specifically märzen's younger sibling, Vienna lager, although you might wish to go to a pale ale if the barbecue sauce is very spicy. For pork medallions in a mustard or savory cream sauce, try a Bohemian pilsner with the hop to balance the cream and the floral body to meet the flavors of the dish. And for just about any pork dish, especially those with brown sauces, brown ale will work admirably as an alternative to the bottom-fermented options.

FISH

Whether grilled, broiled, steamed or fried, whitefish is a natural match for crisp, clean pilsners of either the Bohemian or German variety. The crispness of the beer, combined with whatever delicacies each individual pilsner may offer, will provide the perfect complement to the delicate, melt-in-your-mouth qualities of a beautifully cooked fish.

For stronger fish such as salmon, a beer with more malt will be required in order to balance the heavier flavors. (For all of its bitterness, pilsner is still a fairly delicate style of beer.) Barbecued or broiled, salmon will taste best when accompanied by a roasty dunkel or a dry bock, but when it is served smoked, dry stout is the only answer.

It is a bit of a mystery why stout complements certain seafoods so adeptly, including smoked salmon, but the pairing could not be better. Perhaps it is because the smokiness of the fish plays off the burnt qualities of the stout or maybe it's because the fish and the stout are of complementary strength in flavor, but the marriage works superbly well and it is never a good idea to mess with perfection.

Dry stout also perfectly matches the salty yet comparatively delicate taste of raw oysters, for reasons listed earlier in this chapter — although I must confess to preferring a dry sparkling wine with my mollusks. Perhaps one day I will make the compromise and, as Michael Jackson suggests in his *Beer Companion*, try a black velvet (a mix of dry stout and *vin mousseau*) with a plate of Malpeques.

Mussels and other shellfish, however, do not get the automatic stout treatment. A classic Belgian recipe calls for mussels to be steamed in, and served with, a deliciously sour and inviting gueuze, but lacking such a beer, a white beer will fill in quite nicely at both the steamer and the table. Baked mussels served on the half-shell will taste even better when accompanied by a Bohemian pilsner and *moules marinière* will call for either that style or its German brother.

Lobster and crab are each very delicate tastes and although some will further the stout-oyster relationship to include these crustaceans, I do not believe that this should necessarily be the first choice. If the boil has been conducted in plain, salted or salt-and-peppered water, certainly a stout or porter will provide the same kind of counterpoint with these shellfish as it did with the oysters, but a Bohemian pilsner will match wonderfully, as well.

When the shellfish are being served in the South, however, it is unlikely that the boil seasonings will be limited to salt and pepper, or for that matter, that the foods being boiled will stop at crab or lobster. A Louisiana boil, for example, will normally be spiced with everything from hot sauce to clove, thyme and marjoram and contain anything from onions and bulbs of garlic to sausage links and potatoes. For a colorful mix such as that, a more "utilitarian" beer style than stout would be in order, something that is highly drinkable and able to pair with a wide variety of foods. For a very spicy boil, then, I would recommend bitter or, when the hot sauce has been left on the shelf, a dunkel.

SPEAKING OF HEAT

If you travel where hot and spicy food is served as a matter of course, even if that only means traveling as far as your local Tex-Mex restaurant, you will always find people enjoying their food with plenty of cold lager. While there is certainly nothing wrong with this practice, it is somewhat misguided in that these diners are actually looking for nothing more in their beer than a fire extinguisher, a liquid so cold and thirst-quenching that it counters the intense heat of the chilies. They don't want beer, they want ice water!

It was a Toronto restaurateur named John Maxwell who first introduced me to a different way of looking at beer and hot food pairings. Up to that point, I had willingly subscribed to the cold lager philosophy and because I love chili peppers and fiery hot sauces, that meant that I was drinking my share of cold lager with many of my meals. But that all changed at an annual convention of the Canadian Amateur Brewers Association where, during a beer luncheon orchestrated by John and chef Matthew Flett, I sampled a chicken in mole sauce dish paired with a local pale ale.

It was a revelation! Even though the mole sauce was only mildly spicy (as a mole should be), there was enough pepper there to tip me off to the point that John was making with this match: Instead of cold lager for hot food, why not try a hoppy ale? It was a brilliant suggestion and one that I immediately took to heart and began to practice. Hops and fire...how wonderful!

The reason for using hoppy ales to mate with spicy foods is actually quite simple and for the most part, the same reason wine writers recommend high-acidity wines such as German rieslings to handle gastronomic heat. The key in this relationship is the ability of the ale's hoppy bitterness to mellow the flame of the spice without needing to be served at the lager's mouth-numbingly cold temperature. After all, you are presumably eating the spice because you like the flavor and sensation you get from it, so why would you want to freeze your mouth and your palate with ice-cold beer?

The other reason for the superiority of the pale ale as a mate for hot and spicy fare lies in the fullness of its body relative to that of pilsners or North American lagers, or rieslings. Because there is more to peppery foods than just the pepper, you need a beer that will hold up to the spice not just because of its hoppiness but also because of the presence of formidable character. For this reason, even the hoppiest of pilsners will not handle food heat as adeptly as a pale ale or, if a four-alarm blaze is involved, an IPA with the extra hop and a bit more alcohol to help fight the flames.

This wonderful marriage works anywhere foods are cooked to be significantly hot—Caribbean rotis and jerks, Tex-Mex cuisine, certain Thai foods, the hotter styles of curry and some of the spicier Cajun fare. In retrospect, however, I do not think that the relationship extends to traditional Mexican foods and admit that I probably would have chosen a doppelbock for the mole sauce back at that beer luncheon—but I'm glad that John saw things differently.

VEGETARIAN FARE

Vegetable dishes cover a wide spectrum of taste, from delicate artichoke appetizers to complex blends of flavors in stews, casseroles and vegetable pies. The scope of these tastes is such that an entire chapter, or book, could be given over to their consideration—there is no easy way to recommend specific beers for vegetarian fare and the best course of action is trial and error.

For those who elect to pursue an organic vegetable diet for health reasons—leaving aside the question of the validity of such concerns—there is a very small but growing market for organic beer developing worldwide. Some of these brews are now being produced in the United States and provide a homegrown if somewhat uninspired alternative for the organically oriented beer drinker. To date, the domestic organics are all rather limp lagers vaguely in the continental style, but this will surely change if the demand for such beers takes off as some predict.

For those willing to make do with beers that are not certified organic (does that make them inorganic?) there are a few beer and vegetable matches that will serve as guidelines for pairings made with more elaborate dishes.

Beginning with "A," the artichoke is a tender and delectable vegetable that needs a crisp, light and like-minded beer for its mate, so try a soft wheat ale or a lightly hopped pilsner. For that summer favorite, corn on the cob, select a beer that will stand up to the salt and butter slathered over the cob, but will not overpower the vegetable itself, perhaps a Canadian ale or a light bitter. And when roasted peppers are presented with a generous serving of olive oil, as surely they must be, the best brew to balance the effects of the oil and enhance the sweetness of the peppers must be a steam beer.

For sturdy, green vegetables like broccoli, beans or okra, you will want a crisp German or Bohemian pilsner or, perhaps, a very hoppy cream ale with a snappy but not overpowering body to set off the vegetal natures of the greens. Cauliflower will also land in this same marriage, but when onions rule the table, a maltier beer like a Vienna lager or an amber ale will make a nice partner to the sweetness of cooked yellow, Spanish or red onion, or leek. Served raw, of course, onion will require a much sturdier mate and it will be time to pull out an American pale ale or even an IPA.

Some popular vegetarian dishes that can be happily paired with beer include quiche lorraine matched to a crisp wheat ale or continental pilsner, falafel paired with a bitter or alt, and Italian bruschetta marries nicely to a malty Vienna lager. Beyond these few suggestions — and I confess to having barely scratched the surface of vegetable-based cuisine here — I would recommend that you look closely at the spices involved in the dish before making your beer selection.

THE TOMATO ISSUE

There can be no question as to the identity of the best beverage match for a plate of pasta in tomato-based sauce or a North American-style pizza with plenty of tomato sauce on a doughy crust: it is a young Italian red wine such as a chianti or valpolicella. Yet strangely, when these dishes are presented on this continent, they are often paired with a beer such as an American or Canadian lager or a continental pilsner. This common though rather misguided mismatch only serves to underscore the fact that beer and tomato are among the most difficult flavors to unite on the table.

The failing of beer as a marriage partner for tomato is rooted in the acidic sweetness of the red fruit. Such acidity automatically makes one lean toward a hoppier beer style, but the sweetness of a tomato will preclude that match, as the bitterness of such a beer will battle with the tomato's sugars. Add to this dilemma the robust flavor of a tomato, particularly when it is in paste or sauce form, and the difficulties become even more pronounced.

Fortunately, a little deductive reasoning will soon solve the tomato mystery. As sweetness is tasted with the front of the tongue and acidity is sensed at the back, it stands to figure that the best beer style for a tomato would be one that corresponds to this taste profile; that is, a sweetish start and body with a dry or bittering finish. To these requirements, add the need for a body rich enough to stand up to the tomato's intensity, yet not so powerful as to overpower it, and the choice is reduced to Vienna lagers and maybe certain bocks: Vienna lager with pizza; a light and relatively dry pale bock for lasagna or spaghetti bolognese; Vienna again for ravioli or cannelloni; and either style with goulash, depending on how rich the stew might be. While this limited selection does not leave much room for a great deal of variety when pairing tomato-based foods with beers — heaven forbid that someone might wish to host a beer dinner with a tomato theme — the delicious but forcefully individualistic taste of the tomato makes it a rule that is very difficult to break. When you want something different, however, there is always that nice bottle of chianti.

BARBECUES

In North America, the backyard barbecue is almost sacrosanct in its position as a social or family event. Socially, it allows for casual entertaining without presenting undue pressures on either guest or host, and as the basis for a family meal, the barbecue eases the formality of the dinner table and lets parents and offspring interact on a much more equal level than would ever be possible at the family dinner table.

Traditionally, the barbecue has always been dad's domain, a place where he could handle the cooking without infringing on mom's kitchen territory, and so the drink for barbecued dinners has always been dad's, as well. Here, beer was the rule and for the most part, that beer was dad's favorite brand of big-brewery lager — probably consumed straight out of the can.

But times have changed and so have barbecues. With more men handling the cooking in the kitchen, there is less territorialism attached to the grill. And with the evolution of the gas barbecue, it is now more popular to grill food on an almost year-round basis, thereby removing some of the ceremony attached to the barbecuing experience. Yet two things remain the same: the grill is still tended more by dad than by mom and the beverage of choice is still the cold commercial lager.

The joining of the commercial lager and the barbecue probably had something to do with the former's status as the drink of the working man and the latter's informality. Where pretense was dropped, as it certainly was at the grill, beer could be enjoyed without fear of someone looking down their nose at you for your choice of beverage. There were no stemmed glasses or good crystal around the barbecue; beer out of the can or bottle was good enough for anyone, from white-collar executive to blue-collar factory hand.

As enticing as such an egalitarian setting may be, it is based on the misconception that good taste cannot be casual. Big-brewery lager may indeed be the drink of choice for most working people, but it hardly stands up to the powerful flavors and aromas generated by outdoor cooking. The juicy, smoky and slightly burnt taste of a charcoal-broiled steak or hamburger is surely too much flavor for a thin and sweet American lager, and no ice or light beer could ever survive the seasoned onslaught of a rack of barbecued ribs soaked in sauce or chicken wings coated in dried chilies and garlic. Democratic as it may be, the big-brewery lager is a washout at the grill.

The best and most obvious answer to barbecued flavors, and my personal favorite, is a rauchbier. The roasty, smoky flavor of such a brew will match beautifully the tastes generated by the grill's flames and the best qualities of both beer and barbecue will surely be pulled to the surface. This marvelous mixture may, however, prove to be too much for some as the burnt flavors of meat and brew do tend to add up exponentially. For these folks, then, I suggest a dry porter or stout, preferably one with a roastiness all its own, to act as a milder surrogate for the smoked beer.

If sauces are involved in the barbecuing, you may wish to refer to the sections on hot foods or tomatoes. However, because of the power of the barbecue's influence on food, this should be considered purely as an option. The tomato qualities of a barbecue sauce, for example, may call to mind a Vienna lager, but that beer could quite easily have its taste drowned out by the smokiness of the grill. And to add a touch of novelty to your barbecue, another option to consider is the addition of one of the many new chili-flavored beers currently on the market.

BRUNCH

"Beer: it's not just for breakfast anymore." A joke line, invoked innumerable times during university days, on camping trips and at parties all across the continent — but who's to say that there isn't a glimmer of truth behind this glib remark?

While drinking beer for breakfast may not be the most socially acceptable practice, history tells us that it is only recently that this has become the case. As an excellent source of carbohydrates — literally "liquid bread" — beer has important nutritional benefits (for example, protein and vitamin B complex) that are required for the efforts of the day and so the beverage has been welcomed at the breakfast table for far more years than it has been shunned there. Throughout its 5,000-year history, beer has been a drink for all times of the day and as recently as the time of colonial America, it was commonplace to enjoy beer at breakfast, lunch and dinner.

The people of those eras, though, were likely drinking their beer to fortify themselves for long days of intensive, hard labor, and there is a great deal of difference between drinking a glass of beer before toiling a ten-hour day in the fields and doing so before eight hours of sitting behind an office desk. Yet this need not mean that we should never enjoy the way in which beer can enrich our morning meal, for there is still the weekend brunch to consider.

It was indeed a quirk of gastronomy that decided the Bloody Mary should be the ideal brunch drink. The rich tomato juice is heavy on the stomach, the spices shock the palate and the flavor marries not at all with any of the traditional brunch dishes, save perhaps *huevos rancheros* or a Spanish omelet. Far better is the Canadian-born Bloody Caesar, made with a lighter-tasting clam and tomato cocktail rather than pure tomato juice. Better still is a light wheat beer such as a wit.

The Belgians must have had breakfast in mind when they invented white beer, because there is little in the realm of drink that better complements the first meal of the day. The flavor and alcohol content are light, the spiciness is sufficient to awaken the palate without assaulting it and the spritzy, slightly citric taste marries beautifully with all but the heaviest egg dishes.

There are, however, far weightier brunch foods than scrambled eggs and bacon or poached eggs on toast, and for these dishes, a beer of increased weight will be required. Eggs Benedict, for example, will welcome a light pilsner or a citric weisse to balance the thickness of the hollandaise with its mild astringency, and when heavy cheese omelets are being served, a fairly tame bitter will match the weight of the fillings without overpowering the delicacy of the eggs. The constant here is to avoid any particularly heavy brews — unless, of course, you are heading out to work the fields after brunch.

DESSERT

No other beer and food match prompts as much eye rolling or elicits more incredulous looks than the marriage of beer with dessert. "Impossible," the skeptics say. "Beer could never match the sweetness of an apple pie or the richness of a cheesecake. Surely this is where beer's utility breaks down."

Nope.

In fact, if anything, the post-meal sweet is where beer excels as an accompaniment. The reason most North Americans fail to see this is that they are so attuned to the typical, major brewery brands that they have missed the many rich and wonderful styles that marry so well to like foods. It is an omission that deprives many beer aficionados of some of the finest beer-food combinations going.

One dominant dessert flavor is chocolate, and it is a taste that is virtually impossible to mate with anything but like-flavored coffees or liqueurs — anything, that is, outside of beer. As chocolate assumes many forms, so it has numerous appropriate beers to complement its guises. In a pudding or mousse, nothing will complement chocolate better than a silken oatmeal stout. A dense, flourless chocolate cake will stand up well beside an imperial stout, whereas a sweeter and more airy gâteau will call for a sweet stout or a barley wine. Plain chocolate candies, on the other hand, will usually be deliciously answered by a strong and rich ale in the 10–12% alcohol by volume range.

Berry-flavored fruit ales always provide a nice counterpoint to chocolate in its various incarnations, and some of the more inventive fruit beers such as those flavored with apricot or peach will serve nicely, as well. If the chocolate flavor is too heavy or bitter, however, all but the fruitiest of fruit beers will lose out to the stronger taste of the dessert.

Chocolate combined with nuts can be married nicely with some of the nuttier British pale or brown ales, and chocolate ice cream will pair beautifully with a Belgian-style abbey ale, either at its side or whipped right in with the ice cream. And consider a sweet and strong Scotch ale the next time you are having chocolate flan or cheesecake.

For lighter, non-chocolate dessert dishes such as sorbets or soufflés, Belgian-style white beers will be excellent mates, with their light, spritzy characters and faintly orange tastes. With pies of various flavors, you might like to turn to that same wit or a fruit-flavored wheat beer, and I can think of no better partner for the Cajun dessert, bananas Foster (pan-fried bananas with brown sugar, spice and plentiful amounts of rum), than a traditional banana-y weisse.

A sponge cake and fruit dish such as an upside-down cake or a sherry trifle will be beautifully accented by a beer flavored with one of the dessert's dominant fruits, and a lemon meringue pie can similarly be set off well by a citric wheat ale or weisse. In that same vein, the Christmas pudding deserves a strong, spiced ale that will reflect many of the spices contained in the pudding, although a Christmas fruitcake might better be accompanied by a brandy-ish doppelbock.

With a few wheaty exceptions, the thread weaving through all of these dessert matches is the theme of strength, both in alcohol and character. Just as the liqueurs and cognacs follow the wine to the table, so should stronger beers follow their weaker brethren in the dining lineup, and hence the grand finale should be the presentation of the strongest of all the evening's brews. As well, there will be a need for intense, bold and sweet flavors to answer to the sugary richness of most desserts, so stronger, sweeter ales and doppelbocks are the natural styles with which to end the meal.

CHEESE

If beer has a natural companion food, it must certainly be cheese. They share the same vast diversity of style, the same quirky complexity and even the same monastic background. And like beer, cheese is made in a great many nations, each one insisting that its varieties are the world's finest.

In his outstanding and encyclopedic volume exploring the relationship between food and science, *On Food and Cooking*, Harold McGee quite rightly observes that cheese, like beer, is made by way of a system of controlled decay. In both cases, beneficial microorganisms are employed to break down constituent parts of organic matter, the result being the creation of new flavors in a food that only vaguely resembles the original ingredients. With such a similar creation process, it is hardly surprising that beer and cheese complement each other so well at the table. Hardly surprising, true, but also hardly commonplace.

Most people will be familiar with the wine-and-cheese party, it being a staple affair among certain social groups. The rationale behind this gastronomic union involves the coupling of the relatively high-fat content of most cheeses with the counterbalancing acidity of most wines, and it is enticing logic, indeed. Yet the fact that this same relationship holds true for *beer* and cheese has hardly helped propel beer-and-cheese parties to the top of the social calendar. Once again, beer's oft-maligned image in North America prevents the enjoyment of a fantastic variety of wonderful taste sensations.

Matching beer to cheese would appear to be as easy as falling off the proverbial (cheese) log. Bearing in mind that you want to treat beer's hoppiness the same way as you would wine's acidity, one would think that the making of such marriages would become a simple matter of picking the appropriate level of hoppiness for each cheese, dependent on the latter's fat content. Appearances, however, can be deceiving and this is one place where the acidity-hoppiness relationship breaks down.

The bitterness rule does not apply to cheese pairings because of the diverse and complex ways in which fats manifest themselves in cheeses. A creamy Camembert, for example, might appear to the eye to be higher in fat content than a firm cheddar, but the truth of the matter is that their fat percentages will probably be much the same or, if anything, the cheddar's might be a little higher. Likewise, a mild, melt-in-your-mouth Havarti will have roughly the same fat content as a sharp Parmesan or a sturdy Emmental. Yet none of these five cheeses will taste at all similar.

Partnering beer to cheese, then, becomes almost as much an issue of personal preference as one of rules and guidelines. Having said that, however, there are some beers that lend themselves to certain types of cheese better than others.

Because their bodies are thinner and their characters generally less assertive, pilsners and other lagers will be overpowered by all but the mildest of cheeses. Cream cheese on a bagel with a little freshly ground pepper will make a nice partner to a German pils, but I wouldn't want to make the same match with any cheese of a more forceful personality. Similarly, wheat beers will become lost beside most cheeses, with the possible exceptions of spicy wits paired with such mild, semihard cheeses as Edam or Gouda.

Contrast is not generally a great idea when making beer and cheese pairings; strong with strong and mild with mild is a far better rule of thumb. As with all such rules, however, there are exceptions. One example, for reasons I cannot fathom, is the marvelous way in which dry stout and French Brie make such delicious partners. Also bear in mind that robust sweetness will often partner well with strong flavors, as in the pairing of a strong, sweet ale with a Stilton.

(On the subject of Brie, I am reminded of a hint handed to me by food and beer writer Lucy Saunders. When matching beer to a cheese with a rind, Lucy suggests first trying the cheese with the rind removed before selecting your final beer mate. The reason for this, she says, is that the rind, being a mold, may carry certain enzymes that could adversely affect the taste of the beer. Smart idea, that.)

The mildly aromatic and smooth cheeses of Belgium's Trappist monasteries suggest that similar cheeses more readily available in North America, such as Muenster or brick, will be well complemented by abbey-style ales, and the presence of English cheddars in the traditional pub-style plowman's lunch provides a hint that these cheeses will match well with pints of bitter. Such geographic grouping also leads one to the natural partnership of strong doppelbocks and pungent German cheeses such as Limburger.

Finally, you may wish to try certain fruit or spiced beers with new-world cheeses like Monterey Jack or fruit-flavored cream cheeses, and stouts and porters can be perfectly paired with various blue cheeses simply by following the stronger cheese to stronger-tasting beer rule. And when you think that you have a handle on the beer and cheese relationship, I recommend trying a smoked beer with a smoked Gruyère — perhaps with some barbecued sausage, as well.

PLEASING THE CROWD

In writing about any beverage, whether beer, wine or spirit, comparisons between drink families are somehow inevitable, as is evidenced by the several references I have made to wine in this chapter. Moreover, when presenting a case for the appropriateness of a specific drink at the dining table, weighing the merits of one drink against another is even more unavoidable. In this light, I present here what may be the finest quality of beer relative to the dining table: its unparalleled ability to please everyone.

One of the most difficult obstacles to overcome when ordering wine for a group is the matter of matching one wine to many different foods. Naturally, when dining at home where everyone is consuming identical dishes, the wine match becomes quite simple, but put a group of four in a restaurant where everyone is ordering a completely different meal and the wine order becomes much trickier.

This is where beer becomes even more utilitarian. Because it is generally served in smaller bottles and is usually of much lower alcohol content, beer can be ordered much more easily on an individual basis. And with more easily consumable portions being served, it also becomes possible to match your drink to each and every course, regardless of how many there may be.

Just think, no more worrying about the by-the-glass house wine being oxidized or of inferior quality, or fretting about leaving the heel of an expensive bottle of wine on the table as you leave the restaurant. Even better, think of how suave you will look when you order separate beers for each member of your dining party, *based solely on what they have decided to have for dinner.*

BEER DRINKS

While they are not exactly beer and food matches, there have been countless beer-based cocktails and flavored beer concoctions invented over the centuries. Indeed there are many that we commonly enjoy today, even if we are unlikely to think of them as such.

From the United Kingdom, we have lager and lime cordial, a partnership that Californians modified to Mexican lager with a fresh lime section jammed into the bottle. (In my bartending days, I once served a regular customer who, no doubt thinking himself an Anglo-Californian, used to drink pints of English ale with a lime wedge squeezed and plopped into the mug.) Also of British origin is the shandy, a blend of lager and lemonade or lemon soda.

The Canadian prairies gave us the unlikely combination of lager and tomato juice — a Red Eye — and although no true Irishman will likely admit to its invention, a Black Velvet is a blend of stout and champagne. Far more common, and, perhaps, palatable, is the Black and Tan, a blend of stout and ale. (Several breweries now market bottled or kegged blends called Black and Tans, which are actually stout and lager combinations. These are not true Black and Tans; if anything, they are Black and Blondes.) And of indeterminate origin is the Snake Bite, a half-and-half mixture of lager and cider.

Far more interesting than any of these concoctions, however, are the many beer drinks that have been invented, popularized and forgotten through the ages. The most famous of these was the Beer Flip, variously a concoction of warm ale, sugar, rum and raw egg, mixed through its passage from one mug to another and heated by the insertion of a red-hot fireplace poker. A questionable use of fine ale, to be sure, but perhaps an adequate way to dispose of ales of uncertain character.

What is behind all of these odd and ordinary libations is beer's unwavering ability to bond with just about any flavor on the planet. From Black Velvet to Boilermaker, there exists no beer combination that will not set someone's mouth to watering, or so it seems, and you can be sure that just about every possibility will have been investigated by the time the last breath is drawn on this planet. Me, I'm going to go and stoke the fire for a Beer Flip.

CHAPTER 6

BEER IN THE
KITCHEN

Beer cuisine is perhaps still an odd concept in most North American kitchens, but it is hardly thus around the world. The Belgians and French have demonstrated remarkable aptitude with *cuisine à la bière* through the ages and several of the best pub dishes in British cuisine make good use of ales, porters and stouts. Indeed, beer-based cookery is, if not exactly commonplace, certainly quite popular in most nations where beer is part of the local culture.

Although, as Bruce Aidells and Denis Kelly showed in their *Real Beer and Good Eats* cookbook, dishes constructed with beer were not unheard of in the early days of North American life, many of them fell out of favor through the years as beer was vilified during Prohibition and its aftermath. Today, however, beer cuisine is making a glorious comeback in all parts of North America and lovers of food as well as lovers of beer have reason to rejoice.

As this section will show, cooking with beer is much more than beef stews with beer-based gravy or beer-battered fish and chips. The range of gastronomic wonders made possible by the use of beer extends from breads to salads, seafoods to snacks and ragouts to ice-cream shakes. If the recipe calls for a liquid, there is probably a beer style that can be substituted, frequently with improved results.

The following recipes have been generously donated by many of the fine and personable individuals I have had the pleasure of meeting through my years covering the beer industry. Some of these people are industry professionals, others are fellow writers and still others are the respected chef/owners of several of the continent's top restaurants. Without exception, however, they are food lovers who understand and appreciate the range, diversity and adaptability of beer, in both the kitchen and the glass.

Each of these dishes has been tested in my own kitchen and I can assure you that my wife and I have rarely eaten better than we did during our recipe-testing period. I have also taken pains to match each dish to an appropriate beer style and have made suggestions of specific brands that meet the taste profiles required. Don't take my word for it, though; make them and match them yourself — you won't be sorry.

BEER NOTE

Before opening the recipe section, I feel somewhat obliged to make an important point regarding beer styles and cooking. Many of the beer-based recipes one sees in cookbooks, magazines and promotional pamphlets leave the impression that it does not matter what style of beer is used in the recipes, calling as they do for nothing more than "beer." This is akin to writing a recipe listing "vegetable" or "meat" among the ingredients and leaving it to the cook to decide which specific type to use. It is also very wrong.

Whereas the beer you use in your cooking is unlikely to dominate the flavor of the dish with its taste, the style of beer employed will most definitely have an effect on the outcome. It does not take a genius to realize that a dish made with a cup of stout will have a different flavor than the same meal prepared with a cup of light lager, yet this fact seems to escape the notice of the authors of many beer-based recipes. Fortunately, after a little practice cooking with beer, most home chefs will be able to deduce which styles of beer are most appropriate for which kinds of recipes.

And, although it surely goes without saying, each of the following recipes will be very specific as to which style of beer should be used.

SAMPLING BEER CUISINE

When writing a book such as this, and kitchen-testing so many recipes, it becomes necessary to do some entertaining if one wishes to avoid being inundated by leftovers. This menu, then, covers one such a recipe-testing dinner my wife and I hosted for friends and illustrates how relatively easy it is to put together an impressive and tasty beer dinner.

I must confess that we did not actually have the Market Street Wheat Beer for our meal, but I felt that it would have been a splendid match and so have included it here. Preparation time for the entire menu was roughly five hours, not including barbecue time for the chops, and all of the recipes, save the sauce for the pork, can be found in this book.

Beginning with an informal beer tasting accompanied by light snacks

, , ,

Pumpkin Bread made with Anchor Brewing's Our Special Ale 1993
(recipe by Lucy Saunders, food columnist, Wisconsin)

and

Gorgonzola Ale Soup made with Unibroue's Blanche de Chambly
(recipe by Mark Schiffler, Wynkoop Brewing Company, Colorado)
Served with Boston Beer Company's Samuel Adams Boston Lager

, , ,

Sunshine Citrus Salad made with Hart Breweries Festive Brown Ale
(recipe by Sara Doersam, The Southern Draft Brew News, Florida)
Served with Bohannan Brewing's Market Street Wheat Beer

, , ,

Grilled Pork Loin Chops
Served with a reduction of Niagara Falls Brewing's Maple Wheat Beer
(recipe by Stephen Beaumont, author, Ontario)

and

Fourth of July Potato Salad made with Rhino Chasers American Ale
(recipe by Scott Griffiths, William & Scott, California)

and

Roasted Orange Pepper
Served with Conners Brewing's Best Bitter

, , ,

Coffee

Soups and Salads

CREATIVE CABBAGE SOUP

While at the Great American Beer Festival in 1994, I had the good fortune to be introduced to Tim Schafer by Tom Dalldorf of *The Celebrator Beer News*. Chef Schafer, who then co-owned and created at Creations Restaurant in New Jersey but is now installed at the Laughing Lion in that same state, is as enthusiastic about cooking and dining with beer as anybody you are ever likely to meet.

Given Tim's penchant for cooking with beer, it seems appropriate that he made the move to the Laughing Lion, a beer bar with a menu of over 120 beers! With a selection like that, it seems unlikely that Tim will run out of ideas whether at the stove or penning his "Brew Chef's Corner" column for *The Ale Street News* brewspaper.

The recipe that Tim gave me called this dish *Kielbasa, Cabbage and Red Ale Soup* and used the great Belgian ale Rodenbach in its preparation. Because this is a North American book, however, I tried using Quebec's outstanding Maudite from Unibroue and found that it worked superbly well. You may substitute any brown, bottle-fermented and Belgium-inspired ale if Maudite is not available in your neck of the woods.
Laughing Lion, 40 North Sussex Street, Dover, New Jersey
201-328-1800.

Beer Mate Hearty does not even begin to describe this soup. It is the kind of comfort food that cries out for a cold night, a warm fire and the company of good friends, and that means that it needs a beer that is every bit as comforting.

This is a partnership based as much on aesthetics as taste. Picture, if you will, a fireside table laden with bread and big, steaming bowls of soup, and glasses of pale lager. It just doesn't work, does it? No, for a warming soup such as this, one needs a beer with great depth of color, flavor and alcohol but without the fruity esters of a strong ale. Try a doppelbock such as Stoudt's Honey Double Mai-Bock or Vancouver Island Brewing's seasonal Hermannator.

Kielbasa, Cabbage and Ale Soup

5 cups Belgian-inspired brown ale 1-1/4 L
4 cups chicken or beef stock (canned is acceptable) 1 L
1 cup cider vinegar 250 mL

1 bay leaf 1
2 large potatoes, peeled and diced 2
1 lb Polish kielbasa, grilled and sliced 500 g
1 large white onion, cut in half, then thinly sliced 1
1 tbsp chopped fresh garlic 15 ml
1 head white cabbage, chopped 1
1 tsp caraway seeds 5 mL
1 tbsp salt 15 mL
1 tsp coarsely ground pepper 5 mL
Dash Worcestershire sauce
Dash red hot pepper sauce
Sliced scallions, for garnish

Bring ale, stock, vinegar and bay leaf to a boil and add potatoes. Cook until potatoes are just tender, roughly 8–10 minutes.

Meanwhile, sauté the kielbasa in a large, heavy-bottomed pot and add the onion, garlic, cabbage and caraway seeds. Cook gently until the cabbage and onion are tender and then add the liquid and potatoes. Season and simmer for at least an additional 5 minutes. Discard bay leaf. Serve garnished with sliced scallions. Feeds 6 as a main course, more as an appetizer.

DENVER DELICIOUS

In the last year or two, brewing in Denver has flourished and made the city a legitimate contender for Portland's crown as the brewing capital of the United States. But before Great Divide and Rock Bottom and all the rest, there was the Wynkoop Brewing Company, and it still stands as a perfect model for all those wishing to see a great brewpub in action.

The mind behind Wynkoop's main-floor pub and restaurant, upper-floor pool hall and basement club is John Hickenlooper, a man once described in the *Celebrator Beer News* as an "innovator, renovator and brewery builder." I had the pleasure of meeting John at the Great American Beer Festival several years ago and have chatted with him while dining at his brewpub on more than one occasion since. While the chat has always been enjoyable, the dining has been even better and so, when I went searching for a Rockie Mountain recipe, my first stop was Wynkoop.

This soup, the choice of John and chef Mark Schiffler, is unusual in that it eschews the cheddar traditionally associated with beer-and-cheese soups in favor of the more pungent Gorgonzola. The timid need not fear, however, for the ripe, stinky blue cheese mellows gorgeously amid the cream, potato and onion and the end product is a silky and absolutely delicious soup. *Wynkoop Brewing Company, 1634 Eighteenth Street, Denver, Colorado 303-297-2700.*

Beer Mate Although cream soups have a tendency to make the diner call for a light ale, mellow lager or chardonnay, the character of the mellowed Gorgonzola is still such that it merits a beer with a certain amount of bite. For this reason, I suggest that a fairly hoppy lager would make the best bride to the Gorgonzola groom. Something along the lines of a Samuel Adams Boston Lager or a Whistler Lager will probably be enough to send your gastronomic spirits a-soaring.

Gorgonzola Ale Soup

2 lb peeled red potatoes 1 kg
3/4 lb peeled and diced yellow onions 375 g
4 cups chicken stock 1 L
1 pt American wheat ale 500 mL
3/4 lb Gorgonzola cheese 375 g
1 pt heavy cream 500 mL
1 tbsp salt 15 mL
2 tsp ground white pepper 10 mL
4 tsp cornstarch 20 mL

Boil the potatoes and onions in water until the potatoes become slightly mushy and then drain, saving the water. Puree the potatoes and onions, adding potato water as necessary until the mixture becomes smooth. In the meantime, bring the chicken stock and beer to a boil in a large pot, reduce the heat and gradually add the Gorgonzola cheese, whipping with a whisk to make the mixture smooth. Next, add the cream and, gradually, the potato mixture, again whipping to make the mixture smooth. Bring the pot to a boil and reduce the heat to simmer before adding the salt and pepper. Dissolve the cornstarch in a little water and slowly add it to the soup, whisking gently. Simmer for at least 10 minutes prior to serving. Makes 8–10 portions.

HAVING A BALL IN ALBERTA

Buzzards Café and Bottlescrew Bill's Old English Pub is an oasis of good beer, food and wine in the middle of downtown Calgary, Alberta. Having dined there several times, and presented a tasting to a very enthusiastic crowd on another occasion, I had no hesitation in asking owner Stuart Allan to contribute a recipe for this book. Had I known that Bottlescrew Bill's had held its first annual "Testicle Festival" in June 1994, I might have reconsidered.

As soon as I received Stuart's recipes, I knew that I had to include the Prairie Oysters in deference to that fine western Canadian tradition of eating bull testicles. However, because the Oysters represent the only recipe in this book that I have not kitchen-tested — not through lack of courage, mind you, but lack of ingredients — I have also broken with my "one recipe per person" rule and added the instructions for Stuart's hearty Beer and Bean Soup, as well. In the memorable words of my sister-in-law, you could say that this represents a true "soup to nuts" approach.
Buzzards Café/Bottlescrew Bill's, 140 Tenth Avenue SW Calgary, Alberta 403-264-6959.

Beer Mate As noted above, I have not had the pleasure of biting into the "bull's pride" as of yet, but I have sources who have and they suggest that the taste is like a slightly pungent liver pâté. That being the case, I would suggest that a light, brown ale would be in order as an accompaniment, perhaps the same one used in the recipe or the Buzzards Café's own Buzzard Breath Ale as brewed by Big Rock.

The soup, on the other hand, I have made and enjoyed, so I have no hesitation in recommending a beer. The tomatoes added at the end of the cooking process do present a bit of a difficulty — being as hard to match with a beer style as they are — and make it tempting to fall back on the old, reliable Vienna lager. But this is a soup with guts and I just don't think that a Vienna would do it justice. Far better, then, to try a lightly dry bock with the "right stuff" to handle a prairie soup. Try a Capital Garten Bräu Bock or a Granville Island Bock.

Alberta Prairie Oysters — Buzzards Style

....

In a large pot, add 3 parts water to 1 part brown ale. Season with a pinch each of salt, black pepper, thyme, cilantro, oregano and onion powder, plus one bay leaf, and bring to a boil. Remove the outer skin of the oysters and blanch in the boiling liquid for about an hour.

In a second pot, add 2 cups (500 mL) of water to 2 cups (500 mL) of brown ale, 1/4 cup (50 mL) of sugar and a pinch each of salt, black pepper, thyme, cilantro, oregano and onion powder. Bring to a boil and thicken with cornstarch to produce a glaze.

Serve slices of the oysters on top of lightly fried Canadian bacon and glaze with the beer sauce.

Beer and Bean Soup

1 lb dried navy beans 500 g
1/2 cup diced bacon 125 mL
1/2 cup diced smoked ham 125 mL
1/2 cup diced leeks 125 mL
1 cup diced onions 250 mL
1 cup diced carrots 250 mL
1 cup diced celery 250 mL
2 qt water 2 L
1 bay leaf 1
1 tsp thyme 5 mL
1 tbsp minced fresh garlic 15 mL
1 tbsp salt 15 mL
1 tbsp black pepper 15 mL
1 14-oz (398 mL) can tomatoes, hand-crushed 1
12 oz brown ale 375 mL
2 tbsp sugar 25 mL

Soak the beans overnight in enough water to cover. In a large pot, sauté the bacon and ham over medium heat until the fat is rendered from the bacon (do not cook the bacon to crispness). Reduce heat to low and add the vegetables, cooking them until almost tender. Add the water, bay leaf, thyme, garlic, salt and pepper, and bring to a boil. Add the drained beans.

Cover the pot and simmer the soup until the beans are tender. Expect this to take 1–2 hours. When the beans begin to break apart, add the tomatoes, beer and sugar and simmer for a further 15 minutes. Be careful not to boil the soup at this point. Discard bay leaf. Adjust seasonings to taste and serve. This recipe makes 8 1 cup (250 mL) portions.

A RAY OF SUNSHINE

One of the regional brewspapers for which it is my pleasure to write is the *Southern Draft Brew News*, a bimonthly tabloid catering to the American Southeast. The managing editor of *Southern Draft* is Sara Doersam, a generous and gregarious woman who also doubles as the paper's food editor.

It did not take me long to arrive at Sara's name when I went searching for a southeastern take on a beer recipe and neither did Sara disappoint when called upon. Within mere days of my request, she had faxed to me four very different recipes, each with a decidedly Florida feel to it, and my only difficulty lay in limiting myself to a single dish for

publication. In the final analysis, however, there was no question that this salad prepared with Florida citrus best fit the bill.
Southern Draft Brew News, 702 Sailfish Road, Winter Springs, Florida.

Beer Mate This marvelous salad, with its citric tartness, oniony bite and sweet dressing, is a perfect palate cleanser for between the soup and main course of a meal. Sprite and lively in taste, it welcomes the addition of a beer that echoes these qualities without dominating the flavor medley. For this reason, I would recommend a fresh hefe-weizen with pronounced banana esters to act as a beery, tropical addition to the sun country fruit. Perhaps something along the lines of Tabernash Brewing's Weisse or Okanagan Brewing's Old Munich Wheat.

Sunshine Citrus Salad

2 lb fresh spinach leaves, cleaned and torn 1 kg
1 navel orange, peeled and sectioned, with each section cut in half 1
1/2 grapefruit, peeled and sectioned, with each section cut into thirds 1/2
1 cup water chestnuts, drained and sliced 250 mL
1 small red onion, peeled, sliced and separated into rings 1

Dressing:
1/4 cup vegetable oil 50 mL
3 tbsp sugar 50 mL
3 tbsp ketchup or chili sauce 50 mL
3 tbsp brown ale 50 mL
2 tbsp orange juice 25 mL
2 tsp Worcestershire sauce 10 mL
1 cup chow mein noodles 250 mL

Stir together the dressing ingredients and refrigerate for at least 1 hour to allow the flavors to blend. In a large salad bowl, combine the spinach, orange, grapefruit, water chestnuts and onion. Cover and chill the salad if prepared ahead of time, and toss with the dressing just prior to serving. Top with chow mein noodles. Makes 12 servings.

DO RHINOS EAT POTATOES?

Scott Griffiths is a beer man who wears many hats in the industry. As CEO of William and Scott Co., he presides over the contract brewing of all the Rhino Chasers brands of beer and supervises the two brewpubs the company is building at the Los Angeles International Airport. While this would seem to be enough for anyone, Scott has still found the time to coauthor, with Christopher Finch, a beer guide to the United States and, as I write, is in the process of penning a beer-focused cookbook.

By Scott's own admission, however, it is his wife, Loretta Griffiths, who is the great cook in the family and it is she who devised this wonderful potato salad recipe. A simple salad that is quick to prepare, it has a nice, subtle flavor and a subdued smokiness derived from the bacon. As a bonus, it is just as tasty served warm, at room temperature or cold—I personally prefer it warm on the first day and cold as leftovers.
America's Best Beers by Scott Griffiths and Christopher Finch, Little, Brown, Boston, 1994.

Beer Mate Though Scott would undoubtedly want a Rhino Chasers beer paired with this salad—perhaps the Rhino Chasers Därk Lager—I think that, warm or cold, a Vienna lager would be just the thing to maximize its mellow flavors. As a salad without any strong, defining flavors, it obviously could not stand up to anything too forceful, but the addition of the bacon also precludes any use of soft, light flavors. So, I think that I'll stick with the Vienna lager, perhaps a Wild Boar Amber or a Thomas Kemper Integrale.

Fourth of July Potato Salad

2 lb red potatoes 1 kg
1/4 cup cider vinegar 50 mL
2 tsp Dijon mustard 10 mL
1 tsp salt 5 mL
freshly ground pepper to taste
4 slices bacon 4
1 red onion, coarsely chopped 1
2 tbsp vegetable oil 25 mL
1/2 cup moderately to lightly hopped amber ale 125 mL
1/4 cup finely diced red bell pepper 50 mL

Boil the potatoes until just cooked through and let cool until they can be handled comfortably. Chop the potatoes coarsely as desired, in cubes, slices or half slices. Mix half the vinegar with the mustard, salt and pepper to taste and drizzle the mixture over the warm potatoes. Meanwhile, cook the bacon until crisp, drain it thoroughly and crumble it over the potatoes. Sauté the onion in the unwashed bacon pan, adding vegetable oil as needed, until the onion is soft. Then add the beer and the rest of the vinegar and pour the mixture over the potatoes. Toss the salad with the red peppers and allow it to sit at room temperature for at least an hour in order to allow the flavors to blend. Makes 4–6 portions.

Snacks, Sides and Sauces

COOKING THE HOLY COW

Las Vegas is not exactly the type of place you immediately associate with craft-brewed beer—gambling seems somehow to speak more to bourbon on the rocks or vodka martinis than pints of ale. But that fact doesn't seem to bother the people at the Holy Cow! Casino, Café and Brewery one bit.

Having opened as the first brewpub in Nevada in the summer of 1993, Holy Cow! didn't take long to develop a reputation in the beer biz. They captured a gold medal in the English pale ale category at the 1993 Great American Beer Festival and turned many a head with their bovine-themed table at the fest. And their "Moo for a Brew" slogan had more than a few festival patrons making holsteins of themselves.

I met Holy Cow! general manager Mark Monroe at the GABF the following year and got the feeling that, if asked, he would furnish me with a most unusual recipe. Well, I asked and he provided me with a snack food that is not only a step away from your basic chips and dip but positively delicious and easy to make, to boot!
Holy Cow! Casino, Café and Brewery, 2423 Las Vegas Boulevard South, Las Vegas, Nevada 702-732-COWS.

Beer Mate Mark tells me that they make this at the brewpub as a bar snack occasionally, and so it is not surprising that it cries out for pints of ale as an accompaniment. I would suggest a brown or amber ale might be ideal, one with enough hop to match the slight spiciness of the strips but with a sufficiently malty character to handle their full flavor, as well. Try a Rhino Chasers Amber Ale or a Big Rock Traditional Ale.

Holy Cow! Neon Strips

1/4 cup brown sugar 50 mL
1/4 cup porter 50 mL
1/2 cup light soy sauce 125 mL
1/2 tsp red chili flakes 2 mL,
coarsely ground in a spice mill or coffee grinder
1-1/2 tsp onion powder 7 mL
1 tsp Chinese five spice powder 5 mL
(star anise, fennel, cinnamon, clove and ginger)
2 tsp black peppercorns, ground 10 mL
3 cloves garlic, minced 3
4 lb beef, fat removed, and sliced in long strips with the grain 2 kg

Combine all the ingredients except the beef in a large bowl and mix thoroughly. Rub the beef well with the mixture and layer in a deep bowl or crock, covering with whatever sauce is left over. Place a plate and a heavy weight* over the beef and refrigerate overnight.

Drain the beef and place the strips on racks in a smoker, on the barbecue or in the oven. Cook on lowest possible heat for 3–4 hours until nearly dry. Remove and let stand in a warm place until the drying is complete.

*A heavy weight can sometimes be hard to find, but a margarine tub filled with coins will do nicely. Just be sure to put the lid on or you may end up washing your change.

REALLY GOOD AND BEERY EATS

I love cookbooks. Eating may be finite in its immediate possibilities — as much as you may like it to be otherwise, you can only eat so much at any one sitting — but cookbooks offer any number of epicurean possibilities at each and every sitting. And when a cookbook includes beer in its title, I waste no time in procuring a copy for my growing collection.

So it was that I discovered a marvelous cookbook back in 1993, *Real Beer and Good Eats* by Bruce Aidells and Denis Kelly. Steeped in American brewing tradition yet possessed of a distinctly modern tone, full of enticing stories about breweries and beerhouses and as elegantly designed as any cookbook I have seen, it became an immediate favorite in my collection. Heck, even the recipes were great.

Fortunately for me and for you, Denis Kelly has a longtime relationship with the *Celebrator Beer News* brewspaper, even though he recently departed from his position as food editor, and so I was able to get in touch

with him fairly easily. After a short get-acquainted chat, Denis agreed to release one of his recipes to me and, cheese lover that I am, I elected to reprint this fantastic cheesy spread I had previously presented to raves from my dinner guests. If you adore cheese, this one is definitely for you.
Real Beer and Good Eats by Bruce Aidells and Denis Kelly,
Alfred A. Knopf, New York, 1993.

Beer Mate When you are reading the works of gourmets like Bruce Aidells and Denis Kelly, you would be well advised to take their advice on all matters having to do with taste. As such, I can think of nothing better to recommend for this spread than what the authors themselves suggest in their book, namely a particularly hoppy pale ale like Sierra Nevada Pale Ale or an IPA such as Anchor Liberty Ale.

Well, maybe I will add one little suggestion: a Hart Dragon's Breath Pale Ale or a St. Ambroise Pale Ale would work wonderfully, as well.

Cheese and Ale Spread

1 oz fresh goat cheese 25 g
1 oz cream cheese 25 g
2 oz blue cheese 50 g
6 oz sharp, white cheddar 150 g
1/2 tsp celery seeds 2 mL
1/2 tsp caraway seeds 2 mL
1/2 tsp coarsely ground black pepper 2 mL
2 tsp Hungarian paprika 10 mL
1/2 cup strong ale 125 mL

Process all the ingredients in a food processor until the mixture is smooth. If it remains too thick, add more beer. Pack the spread into a crock or small bowl and let sit several hours or overnight in the refrigerator before serving. Serve at room temperature.

COMFORT ME WITH BAKED BEANS

During the fall of 1994, I happened upon a very favorable review of a new book by Joe Fiorito, a Montreal-based food columnist and poet. That same book now stands as among the most cherished in my food and drink library.

In *Comfort Me With Apples*, Joe writes with eloquence and style not only about food but also about how we take our meals and what they mean to us. There are recipes, true, mixed into the text rather than laid out in traditional style, but the joy of Joe's writing is his wondrously celebratory view of food and drink. Even though I had neither met nor spoken to the man, I knew I needed one of his recipes for my own "celebratory" book.

Joe did not disappoint and in the true style of a Canadian who has weathered winters from the Northwest Territories to southern Quebec, offered me a simple but delicious recipe for baked beans, that most hardy and warming of side dishes. And it is comforting, and does contain an apple. *Comfort Me With Apples by Joe Fiorito, NuAge Editions, Montreal, 1994.*

Beer Mate Although baked beans are normally viewed as an accompaniment rather than a main dish, they are likely to be the strongest flavor on any plate and thus deserve the honor of determining the beer marriage. Care must be taken, however, because in this match, appearances can most definitely be deceiving.

A heap of deep brown beans cozying next to a pair of smoky sausages might be justly interpreted as a call for a stout or porter or even an old ale, each selected for its warming and soothing qualities. As attractive as it may seem on the surface, this choice will only serve to intensify the strong flavors of the food and drink until they reach the breaking point and overpower the diner. No, better to settle on a biggish and slightly sweet brown ale such as Brooklyn Brown or, if you can get your hands on it, the unique, tasty stylings of a Boréale Rousse. The body of these brews will be a match for the flavor intensity of the beans, while a little sweetness and a light to moderate hoppiness will cleanse the palate nicely between mouthfuls.

Joe Fiorito's Baked Beans

2 cups dried navy beans 500 mL
12 oz lager 375 mL
2 tbsp blackstrap molasses 25 mL
1/2 cup chili sauce 125 mL
1/2 lb lean smoked bacon, cubed 250 g
1 yellow onion, chopped 1
1 apple, peeled, cored and chopped 1
1-1/2 tsp brown sugar 7 mL
1 tsp dry mustard 5 mL
1 tsp Worcestershire sauce 5 mL
a few drops of red hot pepper sauce

Soak the beans overnight in enough water to cover them well. In the morning, drain the beans and reserve a cup of the water. Put the beans, the reserved water, the lager and all remaining ingredients in a bean pot or casserole and bake at 275°F (140°C) for 8 hours. Check the beans occasionally and top up with more lager if they appear dry. Serves a bunch.

HEAVENLY DINING

During the fall of 1994, I went on a journalists' junket tour of the breweries of the American Midwest, particularly those located in Chicago and Milwaukee, and points in between. As a part of this trip, my colleagues and I were feted and feasted by the president of the Master Brewers Association of the Americas at a restaurant just outside of Milwaukee called Heaven City. It proved to be a highlight of the journey.

Chef and owner Scott McGlinchey and his co-chef Patrick Schultz prepared for us a meal of which Auguste Escoffier himself would have been proud, with each of the seven courses both cooked and expertly paired with local brews. As difficult as it was to pick a favorite out of such a sumptuous feast, most members of our crew agreed that the delicious shrimp and chorizo cheesecake appetizer was the standout, both in its remarkable flavor and the infallible appropriateness of the beer match.

I was thus thrilled when Scott responded to my recipe request with that selfsame dish. However strange it may appear in name, I can assure you that it is ten times as tasty on the plate.

Heaven City, S91 W27850 National Avenue, Mukwonago, Wisconsin, 414-363-5191.

Beer Mate I am sure that I could try different beers for hours and never improve on the Heaven City pairing of this dish, served cold with a warm sauce, with the marvelous, dark chocolate-tinged taste of the New Glarus Uff-da Bock. The full flavor of the bock matches perfectly with the black bean sauce and the spicy chorizo, while its dry finish sets the palate up nicely for the next taste of the shrimp and mushroom.

If the cheesecake was to be served warm, it is conceivable that the pairing might change slightly, but I doubt it. Try this either way with the Uff-da or, if you can't locate it, the Frankenmuth Bock or Granville Island Bock.

Shrimp and Chorizo Cheesecake on Black Bean Stout Sauce

Cheesecake:
1 cup crushed pretzels 250 mL
3 tbsp melted butter 35 mL
1 lb chorizo sausage 500 g
1 tbsp chopped garlic 15 mL
3 tbsp chopped shallots 50 mL
1/2 lb raw shrimp 250 g,
peeled, deveined and diced in 1/2-inch (1cm) pieces
1/2 cup sliced mushrooms 125 mL
2 8-oz (250 g) pkg cream cheese 2
5 eggs 5
salt and pepper to taste

Sauce:
1/4 cup oil 50 mL
1 medium onion, diced 1
2 tbsp chopped garlic 25 mL
18 oz dry stout 550 mL
1 cup dried black beans, soaked overnight 250 mL
2-1/4 cups light chicken stock 550 mL
1 tbsp ground cumin seed 15 mL
3 tbsp ancho chili powder 50 mL
2 bay leaves 2
salt to taste

For Cheesecake: Mix crushed pretzels with melted butter and press into the bottom of a 10-inch (3 L) springform pan. Bake the crust at 350°F (180°C) for 10–12 minutes, until the edges are light brown, then chill. Sauté chorizo over medium heat in a dry pan for roughly 4 minutes, then add garlic, shallots, shrimp and mushrooms and continue to sauté for another 4 minutes. Drain well and set aside.

In a large bowl, whip the cream cheese at medium speed for 3 minutes and slowly add one egg at a time until they are all fully incorporated. Fold in the shrimp mixture and season. Place mixture in the pan and bake at 375°F (190°C) for 55 minutes or until a toothpick comes out clean.

For Sauce: In a medium pot on medium-high heat, add the oil and sauté the onion and garlic until brown. Add the stout and stir the glaze off the bottom of the pan with a wooden spoon. Add the drained beans, cumin, chili powder and bay leaves and bring to a boil, skimming the foam as it is produced. Cook the beans over medium heat, gradually adding the

chicken stock to keep the beans wet. When they are tender, discard bay
leaves and remove and puree 1 cup (250 mL) of the beans and return
them to the sauce. Stir and add seasoning to taste.

To Serve: Ladle about 1/3 cup (75 mL) of the sauce onto a plate and top
with a slice of cheesecake. Serves 8, either warm or cold with warm sauce.

YOU SAY EGGPLANT, I SAY AUBERGINE

As a side dish or part of an entrée, I thoroughly enjoy the much-maligned
but incredibly versatile eggplant. It was much to my delight, then, that
I discovered baking as an easy and tasty way to prepare the deep purple
beauty.

This side dish takes very little time to prepare, but a fair while to bake,
so planning is of the essence. It works, as far as I can tell, with all varieties of eggplant from the tiny Italian ones to the huge monsters that grow
so easily in your backyard. The herbs and beer used in the recipe are also
interchangeable with others; just avoid using anything — herbs or beer —
that will impart a sour or bitter flavor to your eggplant.

A quick hint about buying eggplant: try to buy one with a smooth,
rounded bottom. Eggplants with dimples on the end opposite the stem are
females and will have more seeds.*

Beer Mates What makes eggplant so great is the way it interacts with the
ingredients with which it is cooked, absorbing flavors and providing outstanding texture. For this reason, I suggest that you enjoy your eggplant
with whatever beer you use in its preparation. As always, however, if you
use the eggplant as a side dish rather than an appetizer, the beer marriage
should be made on the basis of the dominant flavor on the plate.

Baked Eggplant in Honey Beer

1 large eggplant 1
olive oil
herbes de Provençe
12 oz honey lager, or more, as required 375 mL
parsley sprigs, for garnish

Many recipes will recommend that you slice, salt and drain the eggplant
prior to cooking it, but I have found no need for this tedious process
when preparing this dish. Simply cut the eggplant lengthwise into slices
of roughly 1 inch (2.5 cm) in thickness and drizzle each side of each slice

with olive oil. Gently rub a generous pinch of herbs into each side of the eggplant slices, taking care not to bruise the flesh.

Place the slices flat in a baking dish and pour in enough beer to almost but not quite cover the eggplant. Bake, covered, at 275°F (140°C) for 30 minutes before flipping the slices for another 30 minutes of baking time. Serve garnished with sprigs of parsley.

* This helpful tidbit is taken from Sheila Lukins's marvelous *All Around the World Cookbook* (Workman Publishing, New York, 1994).

RINGS OF ROSEMARY

One of the more interesting writing assignments I have had in recent years was for the United Airlines in-flight magazine, *Hemispheres*, in which I was asked to select the theme that most accurately characterized Toronto's restaurants and write about four examples that best typified it. After much thought, and quite a bit of eating, I decided that the ideal way to describe Toronto cuisine was as a "gastronomic tapestry" where chefs pick and choose from the city's incredible ethnic diversity to make dishes sing in several different languages all at once.

One of the masters of the art of blending several cuisines on one plate is Mark McEwan, a chef I referred to in my story as a "culinary Kandinsky." Mark owns and creates at North 44°, an upscale restaurant in uptown Toronto. His food is never boring, always delicious and ever-eclectic; I had to ask him for a recipe.

I must confess that I was a bit disappointed when Mark faxed me this recipe for onion rings, mainly because I still had visions of gustatory glories dancing in my head from my last visit to North 44°. Whatever qualms I may have harbored, however, quickly vanished when I prepared this recipe; the most sublime deep-frying batter I have ever tasted. Sure, it may not be multiethnic, but it certainly is delicious.
North 44°, 2537 Yonge Street, Toronto, Ontario 416-487-4897.

Beer Mate As long as I can remember, I've harbored a weakness for onion rings, but they are the kind of food that you eat without really thinking about it — either as an accompaniment to a burger or steak or on their own as a snack — rather than one you dote on. It is a quality that makes it difficult to match the dish to a specific beer.

Unless you are using these rings as a side dish, in which case you should match your beer to the main part of the entrée, I would suggest that they are best paired with a refreshing, easy-drinking beer, anything from an amber ale to a pilsner. This is a comfort match rather than a flavor marriage and so whatever you feel like drinking at the time will probably be okay. Personally, I happen to be thinking about a Niagara Falls Gritstone Ale or a Mendocino Red Tail Ale right now, but that's just me.

Onion Rings with Beer and Rosemary

1-1/2 cups all-purpose flour 375 mL
2 tbsp fresh rosemary leaves 25 mL
freshly ground pepper to taste
salt to taste
Pinch of nutmeg
Pinch of jalapeño
1/2 tsp chopped garlic 2 mL
3/4–1-1/4 cups Vienna lager or dunkel 175–300 mL
4 eggs, separated, with the whites whipped until firm 4
2–3 onions, separated into rings 2–3
vegetable oil for deep frying

Mix all the dry ingredients in a large bowl and make a well in the center. Pour the egg yolks and 3/4 cup (175 mL) of the beer into the well and incorporate the flour mixture slowly until a smooth batter is formed. If the batter seems to be overly thick, add small amounts of beer gradually until it is smooth. Fold in the egg whites and let the batter sit for 20 minutes.

Meanwhile, cut the onions into 1/2-inch (1 cm) slices and separate them into rings. When the batter has sat long enough, dredge the rings through the batter and deep-fry in 325°F (160°C) oil until they are golden brown. Drain and lightly salt if desired, and serve. The batter will be enough for heaps of onion rings.

A SAUCY VICTORIAN AFFAIR

Although it wasn't the first brewpub in Canada *per se*, Spinnakers in Victoria, British Columbia, was the first one to incorporate the brewery and the pub in the same building. This in itself would be enough to merit the brewpub an honored place in Canadian beer culture, but owner Paul Hadfield will have no resting on past laurels at his establishment. For Paul, the brewpub is a multifaceted community structure and that means providing atmosphere, food and, of course, beer — all of which they do extremely well at Spinnakers.

Although I have been to Spinnakers many times, I met Paul for the first time (in 1993) while I was researching my *Great Canadian Beer Guide* and saw him again about a year later while I was taping an interview for a local television station at his place. Neither of these occasions afforded me the time to stop for a meal, but the memory of great Spinnakers lunches past prompted me to renew acquaintances and ask Paul for a recipe. He responded with not one but four terrific sauces, the most versatile of which is presented below. Don't be put off by the call for oyster sauce; it is easily found in most Asian food stores and once you have it, you'll find yourself using it far more often than you thought possible. *Spinnakers Brew Pub, 308 Catherine Street, Victoria, British Columbia 604-384-0332.*

Beer Mate This sauce is absolutely ideal over barbecued steak, which is how my wife and I tested out the recipe. The oyster sauce, while not overpowering, does come through in the taste of the finished sauce and made my mind wander toward stout as a possible match. However, with the beef at least, a slight sweetness and a depth of malty body were necessary to balance the rich character of the sauce and the flavor of the meat.

The answer could only be one style of beer — oatmeal stout. Try a Barney Flats Oatmeal Stout, a St. Ambroise Oatmeal Stout or a Rogue Shakespeare Stout.

Mushroom and Wheat Sauce

....

1/4 cup chopped mushrooms 50 mL
2 tbsp chopped shallots 25 mL
2 cloves garlic, chopped 2
1 tsp Dijon mustard 5 mL
4 shakes Worcestershire sauce 4
2 tbsp oyster sauce 25 mL
3/4 cup weizen or hefe-weizen 175 mL
2 tbsp brown sugar 25 mL
Pinch dried oregano
5 fresh rosemary leaves 5
Pinch black pepper
1 sprig fresh thyme 1

Heat enough oil to cover the bottom of a saucepan. Add the mushrooms, shallots, garlic, mustard and Worcestershire and sauté for 3 minutes. Then add the remaining ingredients and reduce for a further 4 minutes or until a sauce consistency is formed. Serve over steak, veal, lamb or chicken.

GET OUT THE BARBECUE

I love using the barbecue and will fire it up, even in winter, at the slightest provocation. I also enjoy a deep, smoky flavor in my pastas and so I came up with the following recipe for a rich and tasty pasta sauce. If you want to go the full nine yards, try substituting a rauchbier (smoked beer) like Rogue Smoke or Zip City Rauchbier in the place of the stout.

Beer Mate I have always wondered how beer and pizza or beer and spaghetti came to be such essential culinary combinations, since tomato is one of the toughest flavors to match with beer! In the case of this dish, however, the job is made much easier by the strength of the barbecue's smoke.

This is one case where I would recommend dining with the beer you used in the dish, namely a dry, smoky stout. The burnt qualities of the stout will balance well with the smokiness of the dish, while its dryness will easily stand up to the subdued whisky flavor. If you elect to cook the rauchbier variation, I would still recommend serving the stout as the combination of the dish and the rauchbier may just prove to be too smoky to handle.

Barbecued Stout Pasta Sauce

....

6 medium tomatoes 6
1 green pepper 1
1 sweet red pepper 1
1 hot banana pepper (optional) 1
2 medium onions 2
2 Italian or Macedonian sausages (roughly 1 lb/500 g) 2
1 cup dry stout (or optional rauchbier) 250 mL
1 5-1/2-oz can tomato paste 156 mL
1 large clove garlic 1
1 tbsp dried oregano 15 mL
1/2 tbsp dried basil 7 mL
1/2 tbsp parsley 7 mL
salt and pepper to taste

Lengthwise halve the tomatoes, peppers and onions and barbecue them, along with the sausages, on a medium flame until the vegetable skins are slightly charred and the sausages cooked. (The sausages may be parboiled in advance of barbecuing if time is a consideration.) Remove the vegetables and sausages from the grill and allow them to cool until they can be comfortably handled.

Peel, core and crush the tomatoes in a medium-sized pot and stir in the tomato paste and stout until you have a deep reddish-brown sauce. Mince the garlic and add it to the sauce along with the seasonings. Stir well. After peeling the onions and peppers, chop them and the sausages into medium-sized pieces (except the optional hot pepper, which should be finely diced) and add them to the pot. Simmer the sauce for at least 30 minutes, adding more stout as necessary and adjusting the seasonings to taste. Serve over al dente linguini or other pasta. Feeds 4–6.

Breads

CALIFORNIA ITALIAN AT JUPITER

During the summer of 1994, I headed west to San Francisco to attend the twelfth annual KQED Beer and Food Festival. It was my third visit to San Francisco and the second time I had ventured across the bay to Berkeley, but the first chance I'd had to visit the Jupiter bar and restaurant.

My host at Jupiter was Elinore Boeke, a delightful lady I had first met at the Great American Beer Festival when she was in the employ of the Washington-based Beer Institute. Now transferred to northern California and quite happy about it, Elinore was handling public relations for Jupiter as well as the two area brewpubs owned by the same company — Twenty Tank in San Francisco and Triple Rock just down the street in Berkeley.

With the memory of my terrific lunch on Jupiter's glorious floral patio still firmly entrenched in my mind, I called Elinore to see if she might be able to pry a recipe or two from the grip of the people running the Jupiter kitchen. Happily, she was, and the following focaccia recipe from Jupiter's Tony Donofrio is simple, versatile and very, very tasty.
Jupiter, 2181 Shattuck Avenue, Berkeley, California 510-THE-TAPS.

Beer Mate This traditional Italian bread goes well with just about anything you care to serve it alongside — it will even make a great crust for a sauceless pizza. But as it is an accompaniment, you will probably want to match your beer to the main dish rather than the bread.

On the other hand, if you are enjoying the focaccia with a pasta in a light cream sauce, or all on its own, the bread will be the dominant taste. Therefore, you will probably want to look for a white beer with enough acidity to balance the flavors of the coarse salt and the olive oil. Try a Blanche de Chambly or, for a gingery take on the style, a Rogue Mo Ale.

Beer Focaccia

Sponge:
2 cups all-purpose flour, plus 1 tbsp (15 mL) 500 mL
1 packet active dry yeast 1
1/2 cup lukewarm or hot water (as per instructions on yeast packet) 125 mL

Dough:
1/4 cup olive oil 50 mL
3 tbsp fresh or dried rosemary 50 mL
3 tbsp fresh or dried sage 50 mL
2 cups unbleached flour 500 mL
1/4 cup hoppy pale ale 50 mL
salt and pepper to taste

Baking:
7 tbsp olive oil 100 mL
coarse sea salt

Sponge: Put the 2 cups (500mL) of flour in a large bowl and make a well in the center. Dissolve the yeast in the water and pour it into the well, using a wooden spoon to slowly incorporate all of the flour. When all is well mixed, sprinkle 1 tbsp (15 mL) of flour on top, cover the bowl with a clean cotton towel and let it rest in a warm place away from drafts. After about an hour, the sponge should have doubled in size, a fact made obvious by the disappearance of the flour you sprinkled on top and the formation of cracks in the surface of the sponge.

Dough: Heat the olive oil in a small saucepan until warm, then remove from the heat and add the herbs. Spread the 2 cups (500mL) of flour on a board and place the sponge in the center. Make a well in the sponge and pour the oil into it, along with the beer, salt and pepper. Mix the ingredients in the well and then, little by little, incorporate the flour until a ball of dough is formed. Knead the dough in a folding motion until it is elastic and smooth and no flour remains on the board.

Baking: Grease a 15- x 10-inch (2 L) jelly roll pan or cookie sheet with 4 tbsp (50 mL) of the oil. Using a rolling pin, roll out the dough until it is the size of the pan and place it in the pan, stretching it to the sides with your fingers if necessary. Drizzle the remaining oil over the top and sprinkle with the coarse salt. Prick the dough all over with a fork and then cover it with plastic wrap and a towel and leave it in a warm place until it has doubled in size again, about another hour. Bake at 400°F (200°C) for 30 minutes and then serve warm, with more oil and salt if desired.

HALLOWEEN BREAD?

As a food writer and cookbook author, Lucy Saunders combines her avid interest in beer with her even keener fascination with food. In the past eight years, Lucy has covered the microbrewing movement for both trade and consumer publications, with a special focus on beer cuisine provided by her syndicated column, "The Beer and Food Companion."

I first encountered Lucy via our links with the nascent North American Guild of Beer Writers and, in meeting her, I found a person who shares my enthusiasm for the many ways beer can enhance the dining experience. As one of the first students in the professional baking and pastry program of the Cooking and Hospitality Institute of Chicago, Lucy began her culinary experiments with beer batters and quick breads, and so it is with a nod to her roots that she contributes the following pumpkin bread recipe. Simple as it is to prepare, it provides an exquisite taste sensation fresh from the oven; or even a few days later, toasted and buttered.

Beer Mate As this is a sweet and tasty bread, but not exactly a dessert, the most appropriate role for it to play in your gastronomic life is as either a snack or an aside to soup or salad. In either of these roles, it is unlikely to warrant a beer marriage; even I don't go as far as to match beers to my snacks or table bread.

If, however, you dearly wish to drink something with your bread — perhaps while enjoying it as a light lunch or midafternoon sustainment — try the same spiced ale you used for baking it or, failing that, a similarly spiced beer, spicy (as opposed to spiced) ale or a rich bock. The idea is the same in all cases: Pick a beer that will stand up to the sweet and rich character of the bread.

Pumpkin Bread

....

1/4 cup butter 50 mL
1 cup sugar 250 mL
1 egg plus one egg white 1
1 cup canned pumpkin puree 250 mL
1/2 cup spiced or pumpkin beer 125 mL
2 cups self-rising flour 500 mL
1/2 tsp salt 2 mL
1/4 cup chopped walnuts 50 mL
1 tsp pumpkin pie spice blend 5 mL

Cream the butter, sugar, egg and egg whites until the mixture is smooth. Stir in the pumpkin and the beer, alternating with a mixture of the flour, salt, nuts and spice, until well blended (but do not over beat as this will toughen the crumb). Pour the mixture into a greased 9- x 5-inch (2 L) loaf pan or a 9-inch (23 cm) pie pan and bake at 375°F (190°C) for about 50 minutes or until a knife comes clean. Serves 6–8.

copyright 1994, The Beer and Food Companion

Entrées

PUT SOME ZIP IN YOUR LIFE

In downtown New York City lies what may be the most acclaimed brew-pub on the continent. Zip City Brewing Company has been written up in magazines from *New York* to *Gourmet* to *Paris Vogue* and, partly because of its location and partly because it is so good, it continues to generate press clippings at what seems to be the rate of one every month or so.

Zip City owner Kirby Shyer is a most affable man who fits not at all the image of a high-stress Manhattan restaurateur. Nonetheless, Kirby is the man behind all of Zip City's success, and given the number of New York brewing operations that have either failed or never left the drawing-board stage, he must be doing something right. Certainly part of that something is good-quality food.

Although I have known Kirby for a couple of years, he is such a busy, hands-on owner that getting a recipe out of him seemed at times like trying to get blood from a stone. When he finally came through, however, he explained that he'd been busy negotiating to open a second brewpub just outside the city, a project that, at time of writing, appears to be going ahead. One only hopes that it will be as sublimely enjoyable as Zip City or, for that matter, this fettuccine recipe.
Zip City Brewing Company, 3 West Eighteenth Street, New York, New York 212-366-6333.

Beer Mate The weissbier that is used in the preparation of this pasta may well be too spicy or fruity for the finished dish, particularly if the beer has been brewed with a traditional German yeast. And while the creamy nature of the sauce may tempt you toward a pilsner of some ilk, the delicacy of this dish precludes that choice, as well.

The answer, then, is a light, top-fermented beer as delicate and elegant as this sauce, namely a kölsch like that of Zip City or Goose Island. As these brews are less than commonplace, however, you may find yourself needing a substitute and one of the fuller-bodied American wheat ales will do nicely in this regard. Try Redhook's Wheathook or Big Rock's Grasshopper Wheat Ale.

Fettuccine with Weissbier Cream

1 lb fettuccine 500 g
1/2 cup butter 125 mL
4 tsp minced garlic 20 mL
1 cup weissbier 250 mL
1 pint heavy cream 500 mL
Pinch of nutmeg
salt and pepper to taste
1 tbsp chopped parsley 15 mL
4 sprigs fresh parsley, for garnish 4
Freshly grated Parmesan cheese, for garnish

Cook the fettuccine till al dente, drain and set aside. While the pasta is cooking, melt the butter in a saucepan and add the garlic and weissbier. Simmer the mixture until it is reduced by half, then add the cream. Simmer and reduce the sauce until it coats the back of a spoon and then season with nutmeg, salt, pepper and parsley. Toss the fettuccine with the sauce until it is heated through and garnish each serving with a sprig of parsley and freshly grated Parmesan cheese. Makes 4 servings.

POSTERS AND CHILI

One of the unexpected benefits of the 1994 Great American Beer Festival was that I had the opportunity to meet Jennifer Trainer Thompson, the creative genius behind the Hot Sauces I and II posters for Celestial Arts of Berkeley, California. Not content to confine her design capabilities to pepper sauces, Jennifer was at the GABF soliciting reactions to an early proof of her Classic Beer Guide poster, the follow-up to the American Microbrews poster she did for Celestial earlier in 1994.

Over the course of our conversation, I learned that Jennifer's talent was not restricted to graphics; she was a fair wiz in the kitchen, as well. This delicious chili recipe is from her latest cookbook, *Hot Licks*, and as Jennifer notes, is great for "big football days."

*Hot Sauces I & II and Beer Posters by Jennifer Trainer Thompson
can be ordered from Celestial Arts, 1-800-841-BOOK.
Hot Licks by Jennifer Trainer Thompson, Chronicle Books,
San Francisco, 1994.*

Beer Mate While I would normally recommend a fairly well hopped beer
for chili and other spicy foods, this particular dish has a richness stemming
from its long simmering time that calls for more intensity in a beer partner.

The first time I prepared Go Big Red, the mysterious hand of the food
god guided me to a bottle of Niagara Falls Brewing's Brock's Extra Stout,
a rich and not-too-dry stout in the Irish style. It was nothing less than a
perfect fit.

Other promising matches range from a creamy and muscular stout
like Anderson Valley's Barney Flats Oatmeal Stout to a lighter but still
forceful porter such as the tasty Catamount Porter.

Go Big Red Chili

....

*1/2 cup olive oil, plus 1 tsp (5 mL) 125 mL
2 medium yellow onions, coarsely chopped 2
1 lb hot sausage meat (loosely ground) 500 g
1 lb lean ground beef 500 g
2 12-oz (375 mL) bottles amber ale (light to moderately hopped) 2
1 28-oz (796 mL) can plum tomatoes with juice 1
2–3 tbsp chili powder 25–50 mL
1 tbsp whole cumin seeds 15 mL
1 tbsp dried oregano 15 mL
1/2 tsp ginger 2 mL
1 tsp salt 5 mL
1/4 tsp allspice 1 mL
1 cup water 250 mL
2 14-oz (398 mL) cans kidney beans 2
6 large cloves garlic, finely chopped 6*

Heat 1/2 cup (125 mL) of oil in a large pot over medium heat. Add onions
and cook until translucent to golden, about 10 minutes. Meanwhile, heat
remaining 1 tsp (5 mL) oil in a large skillet, crumble in sausage and beef
and cook, stirring often, until the meat loses its pinkness, about 8 minutes. Drain excess fat.

Add the meat to the onions and turn heat down to low. Add the beer,
and the tomatoes with their juices (breaking up the tomatoes). Add the
chili powder (more or less, depending on desired heat), cumin, oregano,

ginger, salt and allspice. Add the water and simmer for 1 hour. If you like your chili with lots of sauce, simmer Big Red covered, or leave the lid off for a drier dish.

Add the beans and garlic and simmer, covered, until ready to serve, at least 30 minutes, stirring occasionally. Serves 4–6 hungry mouths.

CANAJUN JAMBALAYA

One of the ways I develop my recipes is through a process of exchange with my good friend and fellow amateur chef, Alastair Hood, and so it was with this one.

My goal was to develop a jambalaya recipe made with beer, but I was having trouble finalizing the dish. Rather than continuing my struggle, I wrote it up and handed the hot potato to Alastair, who then made the recipe in his kitchen and added his own signature to the dish. When he returned the recipe, I knew we had a hit. I made one or two minor adjustments and — voila! — the Boilermaker Jambalaya was born.

The best way to serve this dish is with a big basket of cornbread and a bottle of hot sauce in the center of the table.

Beer Match The tendency of many people when faced with hot and spicy fare is to reach for a cold lager. For reasons noted in the food matching chapter, this is not necessarily the best option.

The stout and the whisky make this a fairly flavor-intense jambalaya, so a gutsy beer is very much in order. Although I have enjoyed it thoroughly with a strong Scotch ale, my recommendation would be something more along the lines of a complex, hoppy ale like St. Ambroise Pale Ale or the delightful Pyramid Pale Ale.

Boilermaker Jambalaya

....

1 tsp olive oil 5 mL
2 cloves garlic, minced 2
2 medium onions, diced 2
1 sweet red pepper, diced 1
1 green pepper, diced 1
2 jalapeño peppers, finely diced (optional) 2
2 andouille (or Italian) sausages, barbecued or broiled, and sliced 2
1/2 lb smoked ham, cubed 250 g
2 cups rice 500 mL
1-1/2 cup dry stout 375 mL

1 cup lager 250 mL
3 tbsp bourbon 45 mL
1-1/2 cup chicken stock 375 mL
1 5-1/2-oz (156 mL) can tomato paste 1
1 tsp Bajan-style yellow hot sauce (Mr. Goudas) 5 mL
2 tsp Cajun-style red hot sauce (Crystal) 10 mL
1 lb medium shrimp, cleaned 500 g

Seasoning Mix:
1/4 tsp ground cloves 1 mL
1 tsp cumin 5 mL
1 tsp rosemary 5 mL
1 tbsp thyme 15 mL
1 tbsp oregano 15 mL
1 tbsp chili powder 15 mL
2 tbsp parsley 25 mL

(Note: While I don't consider this to be a terribly fiery jambalaya, others may have tamer taste buds. So, if caution is preferred, omit the jalapeño peppers and hot sauces, reduce the bourbon to 1 tsp (5 mL) and season with cayenne pepper or hot sauce to taste.)

First combine the seasoning mix and set aside.

In a large, heavy-bottomed pot, heat the oil on medium-high heat until very hot and add garlic. Cook the garlic for 15 seconds, stirring constantly, before adding the onions and three types of peppers. Reduce the heat to medium and continue to cook, stirring frequently, until the onion is translucent.

Fold in the seasoning mix until well distributed and add sausage, ham and rice. Continue to cook, folding the mixture occasionally, for 2–3 minutes before adding the liquids and tomato paste. Bring the jambalaya to a boil before adding the hot sauces and reducing the heat to simmer. When the boil has ceased, gently fold in the shrimp, cover and simmer for 15–30 minutes. Serves 6.

JUST LIKE MOM USED TO MAKE

The author of this recipe is a person who I can honestly say I have loved, honored and respected for a long, long time. She is my mother, Jean Beaumont.

The temptation to add one of my mother's recipes to this book was simply too great to ignore; this is the food I have eaten since I teethed, after all, and it has in many ways shaped the person I am today. So even though it took several phone calls before she became convinced that I was serious about using her meat-loaf recipe, which was *her* mother's recipe before her, I finally persuaded Mom to relent and offer up the goods.

I was surprised how simple the directions for this dish were — they being little more than "mix everything together" — and am afraid that its ease of preparation might unfairly reflect on your perception of it. I can assure you, though, that despite its evident simplicity, this is one delicious meat loaf, and that's not just nostalgia talking, either.

Beer Mate I was raised with this dish and have tasted it many times in many different fashions, among them hot with ketchup or tomato sauce, cold with cheese in sandwiches or hot with gravy. So when I speak of instinctively knowing which beer would best marry with its flavors, I'm not kidding.

Even though the tomato content makes it tempting to try a Vienna lager with this dish, the baked beef and onion flavors would seem to preclude that idea. The ideal match, then, would have to be an ale sufficiently mild so as not to drown out the relatively subtle taste of the meat loaf, yet potent enough to stand up to the meat. My instincts say a full-bodied brown ale, perhaps a Pete's Wicked Ale or a Conners Ale.

Mom's Ale Meat Loaf

....

1 19-oz (540 mL) can of stewed tomatoes 1
1 lb lean ground beef 500 g
1 medium onion, diced 1
1 celery stalk, diced 1
1 egg 1
1-1/2 cup cornflakes 375 mL
salt and pepper
1/2 cup brown ale 125 mL

Place the stewed tomatoes into a sieve and gently mash them with a wooden spoon, releasing all their juices into a bowl beneath the sieve and saving the liquid for other uses.

Put the mashed tomatoes into a large bowl and, using your hands, mix in all the ingredients except for the beer. When everything is thoroughly mixed, add the ale and thoroughly mix it in. Place the mixture into a 9- x 5-inch (2 L) loaf pan and bake for 1 hour at 350°F (180°C).

Amateur and professional chefs alike tend to shy away from using very hoppy brews in their cooking, fearful that the bitterness of the hop will transfer unfavorably to the dish. While understandable, this is an unwarranted worry.

In the best of situations, the use of beer in the kitchen will not reveal itself in the predominant taste of the finished dish, although there are limited exceptions to this rule. The beer should serve as a bonding agent for the assorted flavors of the dish, a role for which it is ideally suited and which usually results in the other ingredients forming a taste far superior than that of the sum of their parts. This is to imply not that the style of beer used does not matter, for it most certainly does, but only that the taste of the beer will generally present itself in more subtle ways.

Even with the hoppiest of beers, the above rule will generally hold true. Being a conduit rather than a major taste player, the beer will normally find itself subdued by the flavors of the other ingredients, regardless of how strong the brew's taste may be. Except in the case of sauces, reductions and glazes, where the flavor of the beer will be intensified as the water content is steamed off, a beer's relative hoppiness should not be a major concern to the chef.

PUT SOME MUSSELS INTO IT

You often hear people described as "originals," but find that those individuals rarely live up to their billing. A true original is a person who has achieved something that will stand the test of time, whether through inspiration, effort or sheer perseverance. Pierre Celis is a true original.

When you drink a white beer, any white beer, you can thank Pierre Celis for your enjoyment. Pierre was the man who rescued the white beer style from virtual obscurity and, in 1966, revived it in the Belgium town of Hoegaarden and brought it back to prominence in his native land. Having seen the style become increasingly popular in Belgium, Pierre made the decision to sell his brewery to Interbrew and relocate in Austin, Texas.

I met Pierre at his first Great American Beer Festival, where his new Texas brews quickly became the talk of the show. Between his slightly cracked English and my very rusty French, we were able to establish a dialogue that we have renewed annually at the festival. As I was well aware of how much Belgians enjoy mussels, I instinctively knew that Pierre would be able to furnish me with a great recipe for the tasty mollusks, and my instincts proved to be quite correct.

Beer Mate When the Belgians steam their mussels in gueuze, they serve them with the same beer, and far be it from me to recommend any action counter to the spirit of such a delicious tradition. Enjoy your mussels with white beer; Pierre's Celis White, Blanche de Chambly, Wit or any of a handful of other wits that are coming onto the market in increasing numbers. And enjoy them frequently — this is a supremely simple and delicious dish!

Moules à la Blanche (Mussels in White Beer)

....

2 lb mussels 1kg
butter
1 large onion, coarsely diced 1
2 leeks, chopped 2
2 celery stalks, chopped 2
1 12-oz (375 mL) bottle white beer 1
pepper and salt to taste

Clean the mussels well under cold water. (For wild mussels, this involves scrubbing the mollusks and removing their "beards," where for cultivated mussels, it simply means giving them a quick cleaning.) Discard any cracked mussels or open ones that will not close upon being lightly tapped — these should not be consumed.

Melt enough butter to cover the bottom of a large, deep pot and sauté the vegetables in the butter until they become golden brown. Add 2 tsp (10 mL) of water to the pot (no more than this amount!) and add the mussels and beer. Spice to taste with salt and pepper and steam the mussels until they all open, about 5–15 minutes. Discard any unopened mussels and enjoy with fresh bread and butter. This amount will serve 1–4 people, depending on your appetite and whether you wish the mussels to be served as an appetizer or entrée.

A NOBLE(TON) RAGOUT

Just north of Toronto lies a sleepy little community called Nobleton. Now, I had never really given Nobleton a second thought during the decade or so that I had lived in Toronto, until one summer in 1994 when a friend of mine proffered a menu for a beer-tasting dinner that was to take place at a restaurant called Daniel's of Nobleton. As such events were all too rare in the Toronto area at the time, I was intrigued, and when my friend suggested that my wife and I join her and her husband in attending the dinner, I readily accepted.

The Daniel in the restaurant's name is Daniel Gilbert and, although I didn't know it when I decided to go to the beer dinner, he is one of the brightest lights on the southern Ontario restaurant scene. The dinner was immensely enjoyable and during the course of my post-meal conversation with the convivial chef, it became obvious that Daniel was very enthusiastic about exploring new and different beer tastes and types. I made a mental note to stay in touch with this excellent chef, formidable restaurateur and beer lover.

Because I do not own a car, I don't get up to Daniel's as often as I would like, but that did not deter me from asking him if he would be interested in contributing to my book. To my delight, he agreed and, somewhere between organizing special dinners, maintaining his constantly changing menu and doing everything else that restaurant ownership requires, he managed to fax the following ragout recipe to me. You will be glad he did.

Daniel's of Nobleton, 68 Highway #27, Nobleton, Ontario 905-859-0060.

Beer Mate When I first looked at this recipe and saw the call for five to six tomatoes, I immediately thought of Vienna lager, that favorite mate for tomato-based foods. What I was not considering, however, was the effect of a long simmering period and, of course, the presence of the yam.

As chance would have it, I happened to be wearing a T-shirt promoting a pumpkin lager on the day that I first made this dish and the karma couldn't have been better. Pumpkin beer, specifically a lager like Lakefront Pumpkin Lager (the label of which adorned my chest that night), is a perfect match for the yam, and the spiciness of such a beer can easily handle the tomato and the hint of heat that lingers from the jalapeño pepper. If you lack a handy pumpkin beer, though, try an ale flavored with pumpkin pie spices like allspice, nutmeg and clove — perhaps even an Adler Brau Pumpkin Spice Beer.

Pork and Yam Ragout with Caribbean Stout

2 tbsp oil 25 mL
1 lb diced lean pork shoulder 500 g
thyme and marjoram to taste
2 cloves garlic, minced 2
1 onion, diced large 1
1 jalepeño pepper, finely diced 1

1/4 cup flour 50 mL
1 12-oz (375 mL) bottle sweet, strong stout 1
1 cup stock, made from pork shoulder bone or beef bouillon cube 250 mL
1 celery stalk, diced 1
1 large yam, peeled and diced to 1/2-inch (1 cm) cubes 1
5–6 whole tomatoes, peeled and roughly chopped 5–6
salt and pepper to taste

Heat the oil in a heavy-bottomed pot and brown the pork lightly on all sides. Add thyme and marjoram to taste and the garlic, onion and jalapeño pepper and cook for 2 minutes on high heat. Stir in the flour and cook until it starts to brown. Add the stout and stock bring to a boil before turning to simmer and adding the celery. Simmer the stew for an hour or until the pork is tender.

Add the yam and tomatoes and simmer further until the yam is tender — expect at least 1 hour. Season with salt and pepper to taste and serve over rice or by itself. Makes 4–6 portions.

CRESCENT CITY CRUSTACEANS

One of my favorite cities in the world to visit is New Orleans and my continuing affair with it began as a case of love at first sight. Here was a city that I thought had it all: great food, fantastic music and marvelous culture. The only thing it lacked when I first began visiting the place they call the Big Easy was good beer.

Thankfully, that has all changed now, mainly due to the efforts of the Abita Brewing Company and a transplanted Bavarian named Wolfram Koehler. Abita is a micro that has been brewing continually improving beer since 1986 and Wolf, as Koehler is known, opened the Crescent City Brewhouse in the celebrated French Quarter of New Orleans in 1991. But while Abita beer is generally available everywhere from Tipitina's to the Absinthe on Bourbon Street, Wolf's bottom-fermented delights are only procurable at the magnificently appointed Brewhouse on Decatur Street.

I happened to be visiting N'Awlins with friends shortly after Crescent City had opened, unbeknownst to me. I was thrilled to find an oasis of great beer in the city I loved so well and, in a decidedly unjournalistic but completely touristy manner, told Wolf as much. A couple of years later, I returned to pen a story on Crescent City for *Southern Draft* and found the brewpub, the food and the beer to be at least as fine as it was on my prior visits. Given that great food is a cornerstone of New Orleans life, I knew that a recipe request sent to Wolf would yield something as intriguing as it was delicious, and I was not disappointed by Crescent City chef Mark Latino's take on barbecued shrimp. Who knows? It may even be enough to keep me going until my next visit to New Orleans.

Crescent City Brewhouse, 527 Decatur Street, New Orleans, Louisiana 504-522-0571.

Beer Mate This dish is vintage New Orleans: lots of flavor, lots of calories and the fear-mongering nutritionists be damned! It's not the kind of food I would recommend eating every day, but it sure tastes good once in a while.

Because the flavors in this shrimp recipe are so incredibly powerful — I mean, 3 cups of Worcestershire sauce! — I was originally at a bit of a loss when it came to pairing it with an appropriate beer. I knew that whatever I chose would have to be a fairly crisp and refreshing style, but I balked at the idea of going all the way to the hoppiness of a pale ale or pilsner, lest the flavor of the actual shrimp be lost in the mélange of saucy, hoppy taste. The answer, I concluded, would be a dunkel with a fair amount of spiciness to balance the flavors of the sauce but not so much hop that it would overpower the shrimp. Try a Frankenmuth Dark, a Drummond Wolfsbrau Amber Lager or if you happen to be in the Crescent City, some of Wolf's own Black Forest Dunkel.

New Orleans Barbecue Shrimp

....

4 lb fresh shrimp (16–20 per lb), heads on 2 kg
2 lb butter 1 kg
2 cups black pepper, crushed 500 mL
4 cups Vienna lager 1 L
2 cups dry white wine (sauvignon blanc) 500 mL
5 sprigs fresh rosemary 5
3 cups Worcestershire sauce 750 mL
1 cup Cajun seasoning 250 mL
(several good blends can be found in specialty shops)

Melt the butter. Rinse the shrimp well and place them in a shallow roasting pan with the melted butter and all the other ingredients. Bake at 350°F (180°C) for 40 minutes or until the shrimp turn pink. Do not overcook the shrimp. Serve with plenty of fresh bread and lots of napkins. Feeds 4 as a main course.

BUT DID YOU TASTE THE MUSK OX?

When I was touring the Canadian prairie provinces of Alberta and Saskatchewan while researching my *Great Canadian Beer Guide*, I heard rumors of a new brewery that had opened up north, way north. Considering, however, that tales of breweries in Yellowknife and other parts of the Northwest Territories were not exactly uncommon, I took no great notice of the stories—that is, until I saw indisputable proof of the existence of Arctic Brewing.

As I was on a fairly tight schedule with no room for last-minute modifications, I had to settle for a 30-minute phone call with Arctic Brewing's original owner Vic MacIntosh in lieu of a visit. Full of enthusiasm for his then-one-month-old brewery, Vic proved to be a great interview and an equally enjoyable individual and he so sold me on his project that I am still trying to find an excuse to travel to Yellowknife for a visit.

As North America's northernmost brewery and brewpub, you would have to figure that there would be some interesting dishes being served at Arctic Brewing's Bush Pilot Brew Pub, and you would be right. Vic told me of many intriguing recipes that he could offer for this book and most of them included ingredients that do not commonly crop up on menus south of the 60° mark. What we eventually settled on was one of the finest stroganoffs I have ever tasted and, even if you can't put your hands on some musk ox, I recommend this recipe wholeheartedly.
Arctic Brewing Company, 3502 Wiley Road, Yellowknife, Northwest Territories 403-920-BREW.

Beer Mate I must confess to having made this dish with the beef substitute — it's just so hard to find good musk ox in Toronto — so I don't know what the perfect match would be were you to secure musk ox. For the beef variation, however, I have no qualms about making a recommendation.

The trick with this one is that the creaminess of the sauce would seem to ask for a pilsner while the use of the beef demands an ale. In the long run, however, the overriding factor becomes the general richness of the dish, a quality that is immensely satisfying and requires a like-minded beer. For this reason, I would suggest that a full and flavorful doppelbock would be ideal, with its rich maltiness matching and accentuating the extravagant taste of the dish. Try a Kessler Doppelbock or, if the brewery continues to brew it as they did for their tenth anniversary in 1994, the Brick Anniversary Bock.

Musk Ox Stroganoff

2 lb musk ox stewing meat (or lean beef) 1 kg
1 medium onion, halved and sliced 1
1 clove garlic, minced 1
3/4 cup extra special bitter (ESB) 175 mL
2 cups heavy cream 500 mL
1 cup sour cream 250 mL
1/2 tsp salt 2 mL
1/2 tsp ground black pepper 2 mL
1/2 tsp basil 2 mL
4 tsp steak spice 20 mL
4 tsp Worcestershire sauce 20 mL
1 tbsp garlic powder 15 mL
2 tbsp black peppercorns 25 mL
1 tbsp capers 15 mL
1/2 green pepper, julienned 1/2
1/3 lb whole mushrooms 175 g
1/4 cup cornstarch 50 mL

Trim the excess fat from the musk ox, or beef, and slice into thin strips about 4–5 inches (10–12 cm) long, going with the grain. Sauté the meat along with the onion and garlic in a large pot for 5 minutes or until the meat is lightly browned. Add the beer, heavy cream, sour cream, seasoning and capers and bring to a boil. Add the green pepper and mushrooms and reduce to a simmer. Dissolve the cornstarch in a little water and whisk it into the stroganoff until the desired consistency is reached. Simmer for at least 20 minutes. Serves 8 with egg noodles, half that number without.

A BELGIAN AFFAIR

It is often a meal that is whipped up at the last minute as a result of a spur-of-the-moment decision that proves to be the most satisfying. And so it was when my wife and I paid a visit to the Cooperstown, New York, offices of Vanberg and DeWulf, a company specializing in the importation of first-quality Belgian beers and run by the husband-and-wife team of Don Feinberg and Wendy Littlefield.

Although we were on a holiday trip to the Baseball Hall of Fame, the free-lance writer in me couldn't resist meeting these people to whom I had only spoken on the phone and I had arranged in advance to drop by their offices. This evening rendezvous quickly turned into a hastily organized beer tasting and dinner, however, and we spent the rest of the evening conversing with Wendy and Don over several of their beers and some very fine food. Thus, when I thought of possible contributors for this book, their names quickly sprung to mind.

Wendy tells me that waterzooï, a half soup–half stew, is one of the national dishes of Belgium, a country whose excellent cuisine has been ignored for too long. If you prefer, it can be made with freshwater fish in place of the chicken, and despite the quantity of cream, it makes for a light but satisfying main course when served with potatoes or baguette. *Vanberg & DeWulf, 52 Pioneer Street, Cooperstown, New York 607-547-8184.*

Beer Mate The recipe Wendy sent me called for Duvel as the beer for the cooking and the eating. This made my life difficult as Duvel is a unique beer without North American peer. In substituting a domestic tripel for the Duvel, however, I have found a little more latitude in the beer pairing.

The creaminess of waterzooï demands a companion with a significant amount of acidity and the fragility of the taste cautions against anything too heavy or bitter. Given these constraints, and the possibility of eternal damnation should I pick a non-Belgian beer style, I have opted for a strong, golden and somewhat fruity ale in the Belgian tradition, say, Celis Grand Cru or Unibroue's La Fin du Monde.

Wendy's Waterzooï

2 chickens, 2-1/2 lb (1.25 kg) each, quartered 2
(If you prefer not to deal with skinning and boning chickens, Wendy advises that skinless breasts and a couple of legs will do nicely.)
6 tbsp butter 90 mL
5 celery stalks, julienned 5
6 medium carrots, julienned 6
1 leek, white part only, julienned 1
1/2 cup minced shallots 125 mL
1/2 cup sliced mushrooms 125 mL
1 bay leaf 1
1 clove garlic, minced 1
thyme to taste
4 tsp rainbow peppercorns 20 mL
12 oz Belgian-style tripel 375 mL
3 cups heavy cream (half-and-half may be substituted) 750 mL

In a large, heavy pot, sauté the chicken in the butter until brown on all sides. Remove from the pot and skin and bone the chicken, slicing the meat into strips. While the chicken is cooking, gently steam the julienned vegetables until just tender.

If you have turned off the stove while tending to the chicken, reheat the butter in the pot and sauté the shallots, mushrooms, bay leaf, garlic, thyme and peppercorns until the vegetables become wilted. Then drain off the remaining fat, add the beer and cook until it is reduced by half. Add the cream and simmer the mixture until it thickens slightly. Do not let it thicken too much — the liquid should be milky.

Add the chicken and the steamed vegetables and heat in a 350°F (180°C) oven for 5–10 minutes. Discard bay leaf. In shallow soup bowls will serve 6–8.

EAT OYSTERS, LOVE LONGER

Charles Finkel is no less than a legend in American beer circles. As the founder and chairman of Merchant du Vin, he pioneered the importation of numerous beer styles never before seen in the States and established a catalogue of many very impressive brands. As the founder of the Pike Place Brewery in Seattle, he has contributed much to the Pacific Northwest's vibrant microbrew scene. And as a beer lover and aesthete, he has promoted the enjoyment of beer in its many forms from sea to sea.

These credentials alone would be enough to warrant the inclusion of a Finkel-inspired recipe in this book, but Charles's work in popularizing beer and food matching and beer cookery lend even more weight to his authority. As I spoke to people within the brewing industry over the course of the book's preparation, more than one of them offered the opinion that Charles must certainly be included in the recipe section. The case they made quickly became unarguably persuasive.

Although, through some quirk of fate, I have neither met nor spoken to Charles Finkel, in the end, I knew that this section would not be complete without some offering from the extended Finkel family. This dish, originally prepared with Pike Place Pale Ale, comes from Melissa Flynn, chef to Charles and his wife, Rose, and caterer to all Merchant du Vin and Pike Place functions. It takes a fair bit of preparation, but the payoff is delicious!

Merchant du Vin, 140 Lakeside Avenue, Suite 300, Seattle, Washington 206-322-5022.

Pike Place Brewery, 1432 Western Avenue, Seattle, Washington 206-622-3373.

Beer Mate The beauty of this dish is that it lets the natural flavors of the oysters shine through instead of burying them under layers of cheese and bread crumbs. As such, it should come as no surprise that the finest beer to accompany this dish would be a porter or stout.

My choice, in this case, would be a porter and a relatively mild one, at that. The idea behind this selection is to accentuate the flavor of the oysters without hindering the rich creaminess of the potatoes or obscuring the tender sweetness of the crust. Something along the lines of the Deschutes Black Butte Porter or an Elora Grand Porter would fill the bill nicely.

Pale Ale, Oyster and Potato Pie

Crust:
2 cups all-purpose flour 500 mL
1 tsp salt 5 mL
2 tsp sugar 10 mL
2/3 cup butter 150 mL
4–6 tbsp water or British pale ale 50–90 mL

Filling:
2 lb potatoes (Golden Finnish or Yukon Gold preferably) 1 kg
8 cups water 2 L
3 cups British pale ale 750 mL
3 leeks, white part only, chopped 3
2 tbsp minced garlic 25 mL
2 tbsp fresh thyme leaves 25 mL
1/4 cup extra virgin olive oil 50 mL
2 lb freshly shucked small oysters 1 kg
1/2 cup chopped parsley 125 mL
1 tsp cayenne or white pepper 5 mL
1 tbsp chopped chives 15 mL
1/2 cup heavy cream 125 mL
2 tbsp grated Parmesan cheese 25 mL
salt and pepper to taste

Sauce:
2 tbsp chopped shallots 25 mL
2 tbsp chopped garlic 25 mL
2 tbsp olive oil 25 mL
1 lb mixed mushrooms, chopped 500 g
(shiitake, portobello, oyster, crimini, etc.)

1-1/2 cups British pale ale 375 mL
salt and freshly ground pepper to taste
2 tbsp light roux 25 mL
(equal parts oil and flour, heated and blended to form a paste)
2 cups half-and-half 500 mL

Crust: Blend flour, salt and sugar together with butter, knifing or using a pastry cutter until the mixture resembles cornmeal. Add the water or beer and quickly scrape the mixture into a dough ball. Wrap and store in the refrigerator while preparing the filling.

Filling: Peel and slice the potatoes into thick rounds. Boil them in the water and half the pale ale until tender, then drain.

Sauté the leeks, garlic and thyme in oil until bright and aromatic. Add the rest of the pale ale and bring to a boil. Reduce heat and add the oysters, poaching them until the edges begin to curl. Add parsley and pepper and strain and reserve the liquid. Reduce the reserved stock to 3/4 cup (175 mL).

In a deep mixing bowl, whip the potatoes with the stock and then add the chives, cream, Parmesan and pepper. Taste and adjust seasoning, making sure that the potatoes are light and fluffy.

Sauce: Sauté shallots and garlic in oil over medium heat until the shallots appear translucent. Add the mushrooms and continue to sauté until they appear brown and juicy. Add pale ale and cook at medium heat for 5 minutes. Season with salt and pepper and then incorporate the roux, mixing it in well. Add half-and-half and heat while stirring until mixture becomes bubbly.

Finally: In a 4-quart (4 L), nonreactive baking dish sprayed with no-stick spray or lightly greased, layer half the potato mixture followed by the oyster mixture followed by the rest of the potato. Roll out the crust to a shape large enough to cover the pie. Dot the potatoes with 2 tbsp (25 mL) butter and cover with the crust. Brush the crust with cream and bake at 350°F (180°C) for 30–40 minutes or until the pie is browned. Cool for 15 minutes at room temperature and serve with the sauce.

A WICKED COOK

I had not met Candy Schermerhorn prior to beginning work on this book and, the truth be known, I still have yet to meet her save for over the phone. Her reputation as a spectacular cook and extraordinarily pleasant and jovial individual, however, was well known around beer industry circles and I figured that if all I had heard about her was true, there would be no problem persuading Candy to contribute a recipe. I was right.

The incredibly convivial Ms. Schermerhorn is the author of *The Great American Beer Cookbook* and a cooking instructor in Phoenix, Arizona. Although I had originally intended to ask her only for permission to reprint a recipe from the book, she insisted on offering a unique and hitherto unpublished dish, and I feel fortunate that she did.

This version of the classic southwestern dish was cooked up by Candy for Pete's Brewing Company of the Pete's Wicked line of beers and was originally intended to showcase Pete's Wicked Lager, although any similarly good-quality pilsner will do. The marinade is spectacular and need not be used solely in conjunction with this dish, although it does perform magnificently here. One hint, though: because of the high heat used in the cooking of the meat, you may want to disconnect your smoke detector if you plan to use a frying pan indoors!
The Great American Beer Cookbook by Candy Schermerhorn, Brewers Publications, Boulder, 1994.

Beer Mate I would imagine that most restaurants serving fajitas in the Southwest would suggest gallons of Lone Star or Pearl Lager as a fitting accompaniment. I must beg to differ.

The beer I would recommend for this dish depends rather strongly on whether you decide to use the optional liquid smoke or not. If not, you will probably find that some colder-than-usual brown ale such as Pete's Wicked Ale or Brooklyn Brown Ale will match the medley of fajita flavors quite well. If, on the other hand, you like the smoke, you would probably be better off looking for the complementary smokiness of a rauchbier (Rogue Smoke) or the crisp contrast of a German pilsner (Samuel Adams Boston Lager, Brasal Hopps Brau).

Wicked West Fajitas

....

Marinade:
1 cup steak sauce 250 mL
1 cup pilsner 250 mL
juice of 1 lime

1/4–1/2 cup olive oil 50–125 mL
7–8 large cloves garlic, mashed 7–8
2 canned or rehydrated chipotle chilies, finely chopped 2
2 tsp toasted and ground cumin seed 10 mL
2 tsp toasted and ground coriander seed 10 mL
2 tsp ground black pepper 10 mL
1 tsp liquid smoke, preferably mesquite (optional) 5 mL

Fajitas:
3 lb beef steak 1.5 kg
(top sirloin, top round, etc.),* 3/4-inch (2 cm) thick
6 bell peppers (mixed colors) 6
3 red onions 3
2/3 cup toasted pine nuts 150 mL
4–6 tbsp olive oil 50–90 mL
2–3 tsp kosher salt 10–15 mL

Combine marinade ingredients and marinate meat for 12 to 18 hours, turning twice.

Seed and thickly slice bell peppers and onions, reserving in separate bowls. Drain meat, pat dry and grill, broil or fry at very high heat for 3–4 minutes each side. The meat will be crisp and brown on the outside and very rare inside. Cover the meat and let sit for 25–30 minutes.

While the meat is resting, heat a heavy skillet on medium-high heat. When the skillet is hot, add 2 tbsp (25 mL) olive oil and half of the onions, sautéing until the onions are seared but still crisp. Repeat with the rest of the onions and the peppers and set aside in a covered dish.

Slice the meat across the grain in long strips 1/3 inch (8 mm) thick. Reheat the skillet to high and add 2–3 tbsp (25–50 mL) oil. When hot, add half the meat and half the salt and stir-fry the beef until it is seared on the outside and pink in the middle. Repeat for the rest of the meat. Toss together the peppers, onions, pine nuts and meat, reheating if necessary, and serve on a large, piping-hot platter. If you wish to make a dramatic entrance, drizzle the platter with a combination of 2 tbsp (25 mL) lager and 2 tbsp (25 mL) melted butter just before serving. Enjoy with plenty of hot flour tortillas and chopped scallions and tomatoes, whole cilantro leaves, sour cream and quartered limes. Feeds 6–8.

*Candy notes that skirt steak is the traditional cut for fajitas, but adds that its inflated cost and additional tenderizing time makes it less desirable than a more tender cut such as top sirloin.

copyright 1995, Candy Schermerhorn

Desserts

A PORT (ER) LY PIE

The beer tour of the American Midwest that I took with six fellow members of the North American Guild of Beer Writers in the fall of 1994 yielded many interesting discoveries, beer-based and otherwise. One discovery that nicely combined all of the best elements of the tour, and was fittingly scheduled on the final night, was a visit to Chicago's Goose Island Brewing.

A brewpub operated by the father-and-son team of John and Greg Hall, Goose Island has been a Chi-town institution since 1988. So strong is its presence, in fact, that the brewpub was able to endure a building being demolished around it in 1994, and still be packed on a Saturday night.

My meal that night at Goose Island, complemented nicely by Greg Hall's fine brews, was enough to make me consider them as contributors to the recipe section of this book. But when I received a copy of the menu for a beer dinner that had recently been held at the Goose, I was on the phone to Chicago in no time. Seth Gross, a brewer at Goose Island and graduate of the Culinary Institute of America, was good enough to endure countless computer glitches to get this unique pumpkin pie recipe to me. And it was worth every glitch.

Goose Island Brewing Company, 1800 North Clybourn, Chicago, Illinois 312-915-0075.

Beer Mate This delicious pumpkin pie is unlikely to taste like any other you may previously have come across, what with its gingerbread crust and almost custard-like filling. Nonetheless, it is pumpkin pie and what is pumpkin pie without whipped cream, right?

On that second point, Seth suggests that the porter you use in the pie can also be used to flavor the whipped cream by slowly adding a bit at a time into the cream while it is being whipped. If you opt for this tasty option, you will be well advised to enjoy your pie with that selfsame porter, perhaps Goose Island's own Old Clybourn Porter or that of their crosstown competition, Chicago Brewing's Big Shoulders Porter. Naked of cream, however, I would suggest that a sweet porter or stout such as Royal Stout from Carib or Okanagan Old English Porter would be more appropriate.

Gingerbread Crust Pumpkin Pie

Crust:
6 tbsp butter 90 mL
1/2 cup sugar 125 mL
1 egg 1
1/4 cup molasses 50 mL
1 tsp vinegar 5 mL
Pinch of salt
1-3/4 cups all-purpose flour 425 mL
3/4 tsp baking soda 4 mL
1 tsp ginger 5 mL
1/4 tsp cinnamon 1 mL
Pinch of ground cloves

Filling:
1-3/4 cups pumpkin puree 425 mL
1/2 cup heavy cream 125 mL
1/2 cup sour cream 125 mL
3/4 cup (550 mL) porter, reduced from 18 oz (175 mL)
1 cup sugar 250 mL
4 eggs, beaten 4
4 tsp clover honey 20 mL
3 tbsp finely chopped candied ginger 50 mL
Pinch of allspice
1/4 tsp ground cloves 1 mL
1/2 tsp salt 2 mL
1/2 tsp nutmeg 2 mL
3/4 tsp cinnamon 4 mL

(Seth recommends baking the flesh of a 5-lb (2.2 kg) pumpkin until soft and processing it to produce the pumpkin puree for the filling, but less industrious souls can use canned pumpkin if they prefer.)

To make the crust, first cream the butter and sugar. Then add the egg, molasses, vinegar and salt and mix well. Combine the dry ingredients and stir into the wet until a dough is formed and let the dough sit in the refrigerator for about an hour.

To make the filling, mix the pumpkin, cream and sour cream until blended. Then add the reduced porter, sugar, beaten eggs, honey, candied ginger and spices and mix well.

Roll out the crust with a rolling pin on a well-floured surface until it is large enough to evenly cover a 10-inch (25 cm) pie pan. Gently press the dough into the pie pan and pour in the filling. Cover the exposed edges of the crust with aluminum foil or a crust guard to prevent it from burning. Bake at 375°F (190°C) for 10 minutes before reducing the temperature to 350°F (180°C) and cooking for 40 more minutes or until a toothpick comes out clean. (You may have to remove the crust guard about 10 minutes before the pie is done in order to brown the edges.)

SHAKE IT UP

One part of the repast that people do not generally associate with beer is dessert. Sure, we understand dessert wines such as icewine or sauterne and warm to the thought of liqueurs with coffee and cake at the end of a meal, but beer? It just doesn't pan out for most of us.

Which is a great pity. Because beer and dessert, or beer in dessert, can be a thoroughly enjoyable sweet treat that settles the stomach, promotes digestion and generally makes one feel quite content. That we seldom think of it in those terms is simply another testament to how much North Americans have suffered gastronomically while under the control of the major breweries and their limited selection of beer styles.

There are, to be sure, many ways in which beer may form a pleasant part of dessert, but one of my favorites is the simple beer shake. It was first introduced to me through the written word of beer writer and beer and chocolate pioneer Fred Eckhardt and later introduced to my table by the bar and management staff of The Horse and Plow pub at The American Club in Kohler, Wisconsin. As a taste sensation, it is pure delight and as a digestif, it stands in exclusive company as one of the best.

All one requires for a beer shake is a sweet, full-bodied beer, a few scoops of complementarily flavored ice cream and a blender. Simply pop the ice cream into the blender, add a few splashes of beer and blend, gradually adding more beer until the shake is smooth and of the desired thickness. It may sound strange — my own family thought it odd until I made it for them — but it is absolutely delicious!

Here are a few beer-ice cream combinations to start you off:
- Pumpkin ale and vanilla
- Sweet stout and chocolate or heavenly hash
- Chocolaty porter and maple or coffee
- Fruity, Belgian-style tripel and vanilla or peach
- Strong Belgian-style ale and chocolate

A RECIPE CARVED IN GRANITE

Every region of North America has its brewing pioneers: John Mitchell in western Canada, Fritz Maytag and, later, Jack McAuliffe in California, William Newman in the eastern United States and Ed McNally on the prairies. And in the maritime provinces of Canada, it was Kevin Keefe.

Kevin's Granite Brewing Company has been a Halifax, Nova Scotia, institution since he first established it in Gingers, a tavern he owned in the mid-1980s. Later that decade, Kevin moved the business and finally named his bar after his brewery, and in the early part of the 1990s, he and his brother, Ron, brought the business westward by setting up a second Granite in Toronto. Now, in the mid-1990s, the Granite is on the move again as Kevin sets out to establish a second pub in Halifax and move his brewery to a site that can serve both locales.

The constant in all of Kevin's professional restlessness has been quality food and drink, and a nice place in which to enjoy them. This made him a natural as my East Coast food contributor and I was delighted that he managed to come up with the recipe for the stout cake that I had enjoyed several times at the Granites. Considering its lengthy absence from the Specials board at the Toronto Granite, baking it myself may be the only way I'll be able to enjoy it again.

The Granite Brewery, 1222 Barrington Street, Halifax, Nova Scotia
902-422-4954.
The Granite Brewery, 245 Eglinton Avenue East, Toronto, Ontario
416-322-0723.

Beer Mate Un-iced, this cake quite resembles a spice cake and I have enjoyed a small piece of it with my morning coffee on more than one occasion. (At my home, of course; I rarely have breakfast at the Granite.) As the light-tasting cake makes such an ideal match for coffee, its complementary beer would obviously be one that emulated some of coffee's flavor profile, and, to my mind, that means stout or porter.

Try this delicious cake with a dry stout, perhaps the one you used in its creation, or a porter from the stronger-tasting end of that style. If you are too far from either Granite, your choice could be a Deschutes Black Butte Porter, a Kennebunk Blue Fin Stout or a Niagara Falls Brock's Extra Stout. If, however, you want to ice your cake for dessert, step up the sweetness a bit with a Brooklyn Black Chocolate Stout or Gray's Classic Oatmeal Stout.

Stout Cake

2 eggs 2
1-1/2 cups vegetable oil 375 mL
2-1/2 cups all-purpose flour 625 mL
1 cup sugar 250 mL
1 tbsp baking powder 15 mL
1/2 tsp salt 2 mL
1/2 cup orange juice 125 mL
3/4 cup stout 175 mL
1 cup raisins 250 mL
1 tsp ginger 5 mL
1-1/2 tsp cinnamon 7 mL
grated rind of 1/2 orange

In a large bowl beat together the eggs and vegetable oil. In a separate bowl, mix together the flour, sugar, baking powder and salt. Combine the orange juice and stout in a separate bowl or glass.

In alternating thirds, add the flour mixture and the stout mixture to the eggs and oil, stirring thoroughly. When that is well mixed, stir in the raisins, spices and orange rind. Mix thoroughly and pour into a greased 10-inch (3 L) springform pan. Bake at 400°F (200°C) for 50 minutes or until a knife comes clean. Makes 12 portions, more or less.

CHAPTER 7

··

TO BOLDLY GO...

A s you have probably gathered by now, I believe beer to be one of the most, if not *the* most, adaptable beverages on the planet. From the dinner table to the brunch buffet and the patio to the bedroom, beer can do it all—or so I devoutly believe.

This uncompromising belief in the glories of beer has sometimes led me to some rather odd pairings and conclusions, and occasionally overwhelms my better judgment on where to draw the line when it comes to such pursuits. That is where this chapter comes in.

Over the years, I have matched beer to virtually everything but the kitchen sink, either in my imagination or, once in a while, in print for the whole world to see. I have no regrets, however, and am either proud or reckless enough to repeat some of these oddball assertions here. If there are any doubts lingering in your mind about how magically beer meshes with tastes, occasions and ideas, this chapter should put them to rest once and for all.

BEER AND BASEBALL

When I was but a young lad growing up in Montreal, the Expos became the very first Major League baseball team in Canada. It was to be an event that would change my attitude toward sport in general and baseball in particular.

I like to say that I grew up at Jarry Park, the Expos' first stadium, even though it is obviously stretching the truth. The reality is that I did spend many a weekend in the bleachers at the old ballpark and, whether running around in the stands buying all sorts of junk food or actually watching the game, I remember loving every minute of it. The initiator of these weekend baseball afternoons was my father, a devout fan, and the torch of his great passion for the game was soon passed to his youngest child — me.

It was not until many years later, after I had been weaned from the Expos to the Toronto Blue Jays, that it occurred to me that baseball is

MAJOR LEAGUE BREWPUBS

Andy Musser is a veteran sportscaster and the radio voice of the Philadelphia Phillies baseball club. He is also a huge fan of craft-brewed beer and a man who knows full well the value of beer hunting as a diversion from the tedium of life on the road.

I first met Andy in the summer of 1994 when both the Phillies and I were visiting San Francisco, although not together. The site of our meeting was the hospitality lounge of the Anchor Brewery, where I was chatting to Anchor executive Phil Rogers about the way beer tasting can be an antidote to the loneliness of business travel. Phil was in the middle of telling me about a sportscaster he knew who enjoyed exploring brewpubs while traveling with the team when, as if on cue, Andy strolled into the room.

Personal priorities being as individual as they are, Andy was as pleased to meet a beer writer as I was to meet a baseball broadcaster and we immediately hit it off. Later on, over lunch at San Francisco's stylish Gordon Biersch Brewery Restaurant, Andy described to me his philosophy regarding beer.

In a curious inversion of interests, I found out that Andy "collects" brewpubs much in the way that I try to "collect" ballparks, counting up all those visited and striving to increase that number whenever possible. Of course, most of Andy's beer hunting occurs when he is on road trips with the Phillies and so, he says, helps to relieve the tedium of having to live in a new city every three to four days. It is a method of boredom aversion that Andy swears by.

And Andy is not the only one to have discovered this form of distraction. According to him, there are several baseball players in the majors who enjoy visiting craft-brewing establishments from time to time. And it's not only athletes who are getting into beer hunting; I continually hear reports from beer-bar and brewpub owners and employees about traveling business people who come to their establishments to learn about the local brews. This beer-hunting thing really seems to be catching on.

Maybe somebody should tell our local tourism boards...

analogous to beer. I found that the relationship between beer and ball extended beyond the way that having a beer at the ballpark is as natural as fishing off a pier or skating on a frozen pond. These two great North American passions share so many traits that they can almost be called attitudinal siblings, each one being reflective, subtle and exciting in its own way. More than just complementing baseball, beer actually embodies the game.

This relationship is perhaps best reflected in the different way that beer and baseball are perceived by casual and ardent admirers. Anyone with even a marginal interest in the sport can enjoy the spectacle of a baseball game — the excitement of a power hitter knocking the ball out of the park, the thrill of a fleet-footed base runner taking off to steal third, and making it, or the wonder of an outfielder performing seemingly impossible gymnastics to grab a sinking fly ball off the turf. These are the simple but obvious plays that make baseball fun to watch for everyone, young and old, male and female. Likewise, the quenching taste of an ice-cold lager on a steaming hot day is a sensation that requires little of the person experiencing it. The feeling of a frosty, refreshing and pleasingly bitter beer coursing down a parched throat is enough to make a beer believer out of even the most devout skeptic.

But just as a knowledge of the intricacies and nuances of baseball contributes tremendously to the enjoyment of the game, so, too, does an understanding of the complexities and subtleties of beer help in the appreciation of the brew. For an illustration of this symmetry between baseball diamond and pint glass, one need look only as far as that classic baseball showdown, the pitchers' duel.

Many baseball fans will become quickly bored with a pitchers' duel in which few runs are scored because they only appreciate the big plays — the home run, the batting rally or the line-drive triple to the corner. The low-scoring game, they say, is uninteresting because nothing is happening. The fan familiar with all of baseball's little idiosyncracies, on the other hand, will be fascinated watching a pitchers' duel. He or she will note the different ways in which the batters try to "solve" the pitcher each time they step to the plate and will marvel at the tenacity of the pitchers themselves, even while searching endlessly for any little sign of tiredness in the hurler's arm.

Similarly, beer drinkers unfamiliar with the particulars of different brewing styles and variations will be more apt to dismiss a given beer simply because it does not taste as they expect it to. The stout, they say, is not good because it lacks the light, refreshing qualities they expect from a beer. The aficionado with a strong grasp of beer's many forms, on the other hand, will understand that a stout is not meant to be refreshing. He or she will be intrigued by the complexities and depth of flavor offered by that style of beer and will try to find the various flavors that may be present in the beer, even while critiquing the brew at every sip.

As an aficionado of beer and baseball alike, I derive a great deal of pleasure from the artistry of both brewer and shortstop. And so it was that, in 1993 — at the beginning of the third year of my biweekly beer column for *The Toronto Star* — I found myself bit by the spring beer and spring training bugs at the very same time. Impulsively, I decided that the best way to cope with this mix of passions would be to celebrate the opening of the baseball season with a column matching American League teams with appropriate beers. It turned out to be one of my most popular columns ever.

Some of the pairings I made were whimsical, others based in geography and still others rooted in the temperaments of the teams. The then-champion Blue Jays, for example, were paired with the perennial champion ale, Duvel from Belgium, while the sad California Angels were partnered with Busch Draft Light to produce a similar, if inverse, relationship. The Cleveland Indians were, at the time, a young team with a lot of talent and enormous potential, so I matched them to a Thomas Hardy's Ale, a beer designed to reach its peak after some aging; the Milwaukee Brewers were awarded the commercial lager, Milwaukee's Best, for no reason other than the descriptive nature of the beer's name; and the Detroit Tigers, a team that had plenty of power but little subtlety, twinned nicely, I thought, with any mainstream American malt liquor. Time and space limitations prevented me from expanding my philosophizing to the National League.

As I write this, the miserable baseball strike of 1994–1995 is continuing with no end yet in sight, and so updating these matches is unfortunately impossible. (It is tempting, though, to saddle all of Major League baseball, owners and players alike, with a gallon or two of infected, over-aged and skunky home brew, the perfect drink to suit their current attitudes.) Some day, however, the strike will end and baseball will again be played in Major League parks across the continent. When that happens, I will surely be at it again, choosing just the right beer for just the right non-replacement ball club.

BEER AND MUSIC

One of the more questionable assignments I have initiated over the years was one I wrote for *All About Beer Magazine* in which I matched musical styles to beer styles. As it turned out, the partnering was much more difficult than I'd first imagined.

It may seem a bit of a stretch to match beer styles to musical styles and artists, and it probably is, but there have been numerous times when, while listening to a particular musician, I have felt myself developing a strong craving for a particular type of beer. It doesn't matter if it happens to be blues, classical, reggae, jazz or any of the dozens of other styles of music I enjoy, sometimes a particular tune simply cries out for a specific beer.

I first noticed the music-beer relationship in a tangible way when I received as a gift from a friend a recording called *The Wellpark Suite*, a six-movement Scottish symphony composed by Billy Jackson and commissioned by the United Kingdom brewer Bass to commemorate the centennial anniversary of their Tennent's Lager in 1985. Being a celebration of beer, it was no surprise that two of the movements were entitled "The Brewing" and "Fermentation," but what was eye- and ear-opening was the way in which these pieces of music aurally echoed their namesake processes. Beer, or at least brewing, could be music, as well!

From that point of awakening, I proceeded to yank records, cassettes and compact discs from my collection at random in an attempt to marry musical styles of all sorts to appropriate beers. It certainly sounded easy enough, and at first it was, but what I had neglected to enter into the equation was the fact that there are at least as many, if not many more, styles of music as there are styles of beer.

In the *All About Beer* story, I was scarcely able to scratch the surface of the astounding array of appropriate beer and music marriages. To begin, I took an old recording of the traditional, percussion-heavy music of the Fra-Fra tribesmen of Ghana and mated it with the Anchor Brewing Company's experimental Ninkasi, a beer brewed according to ancient Sumerian techniques. It may not have been a perfect representation of the roots of music and beer, but it was the best I could do in 1994.

After the Fra-Fra drummers, I turned to numerous different types of tunes selected from my collection and attempted to make sense of a beer match for each one. I paired the deeply spiritual sounds of Bob Marley's *Uprising* album with the equally pious and reflective flavor of Chimay Grande Reserve, a spectacular ale brewed by Belgian Trappist monks. I then matched the spicy, spritzy Celis White to the joyous and uptempo sounds of the Gipsy Kings and mated Lightnin' Hopkins's unique brand of talking blues to a classic best bitter, opting for a "session" beer to complement the late bluesman's legendary storytelling ways. Finally, after several other matches, I ended the exercise with a flourish and selected an imperial stout to accompany *Opus 49* of Tchaikovsky's spectacular *1812 Overture*, thus acknowledging the Tsarist pedigree of both music and beer.

Since the publication of that story, I have occasionally dwelled on all of the musical possibilities I missed through lack of space and time and, coincidentally, have come across a pair of stories that also dealt with beer and music, albeit in promotional rather than aesthetic terms. One of these pieces, written by Daria Labinsky for *American Brewer* magazine, brought to mind the all-too-familiar quandary of great music festivals being supplied by less-than-inspiring breweries. It is a dilemma I face whenever I head south to attend my favorite musical festival, the New Orleans Jazz and Heritage Festival.

Like most music festivals, the New Orleans Jazz Fest is reliant on commercial sponsorship for its financing. This is a fact of life for such events and anyone who is of a mind to attend them with any frequency is advised to get used to the idea, as I have. When it comes to beer, however, certain sponsorships become a little hard to take.

Each time I've visited the jazz fest, the sponsoring brewery has been Miller and the available beers limited to the more commercially oriented products of that brewery, such as Lite and Miller Genuine Draft. Now, at the best of times, this selection would be extremely restrictive, but at the jazz fest it assumes Alcatraz-like proportions.

To understand how serious the beer selection problem is at the New Orleans Jazz Fest, one must first understand that it is a music festival unlike any other. At the Louisiana Fair Grounds Race Track, where the fest is held, 11 stages operate simultaneously, pumping out the music of hundreds of musicians in styles ranging from traditional New Orleans jazz to Latin salsa and South African township jive to Chicago blues. In addition, dozens of specialty food booths turn out some of the best-tasting "fast food" you will likely find anywhere, and arts and culture displays showcase the crafts and artistry of many skilled artisans. In such a milieu, can you imagine confining yourself to one beer?

Each year that I am unable to attend the fest for one reason or another, I fantasize about being there, and insofar as it is just a dream, I allow myself to imagine being able to switch beers freely as I wander from stage to stage of exceptional music. A softly spicy Vienna lager like Quebec's Belle Gueulle for Aaron Neville's silken vocals; the Crescent City Brewhouse's crisp and pure pilsner for the vibrant, a cappella clarity of the Dixie Cups; a rich and meditative Gray's Oatmeal Stout for the transcendent sounds of Ali Farka Toure; and a flat-out enjoyable amber ale like the Arapahoe Amber brewed by Denver's Great Divide Brewing Company for the equally joyful rhythms of the Dirty Dozen Brass Band. Why, I could roam the Fair Grounds all day long and never run out of beer styles! Or, at least, I could in my dreams.

THE MARRIAGE OF COUSINS

Having attended more than my share of beer tastings, from stuffily formal to unapologetically casual, a few stand out in my mind as stunningly brilliant affairs. Certainly the time I flew to Emmaus, Pennsylvania, for a tasting of eight vintages of the great Thomas Hardy's Ale remains etched in my memory, as do the remarkable beer and chocolate tasting I hosted at Vancouver's Fogg N' Suds beer bar and restaurant and the phenomenal beer-tasting dinner I and six fellow beer writers enjoyed at the Heaven City restaurant in Mukwonago, Wisconsin, hosted by the Master Brewers of the Americas. For sheer explorational pleasure, however, few events can touch the beer and malt whisky tasting I organized in aid of a story I wrote for *Beer: the Magazine.*

In the story, I described the tasting as "a sort of barley family reunion," and I still cannot think of a more apt title, because beer and Scottish whisky really are family or at least cousins of the grain stalk with the same barley bloodline. In fact, the two beverages are so closely related that the fermented but as yet undistilled liquid that goes on to become whisky is referred to as "beer." Thus, it seems perfectly logical that beer lovers should be scotch whisky aficionados, as well.

For years I have harbored a partiality for single malt Scottish whisky — that which is the product of a single Scottish distillery and unadulterated by any addition of grain spirits — and thought it a perfectly natural goal to seek the ultimate in whisky and beer pairings. As often happens with such "simple" endeavors, however, it turned out to be much more of a challenge than I had originally foreseen.

My odyssey began with a month or more spent searching for appropriate whiskies and brews and deciding which flavor characteristics would be the most likely to work in such a match. I knew from experience, for example, that all but the most forceful of lagers would be overpowered by the pronounced flavors of the whiskies, but I hadn't a sense of how much potency would be necessary in a bottom-fermented brew. Likewise, I suspected that extremely hoppy ales such as those of the American pale ale variety would clash with the dry characters of the whiskies, but did not know how much hop would be too much.

On the whisky side of the ledger, I believed that the softer and more delicate whiskies of the Lowlands might be best suited to relatively less bombastic brews such as strong lagers or best bitters, but had to decide on the degree of subtlety I wanted from the malt(s) I elected to represent that region. And as much as I love the peaty and intense malts of Islay, I worried that they would prove to be too overpowering for any beer, regardless of type. The preparation for this tasting proved to be more extensive than any I had hosted before, or since.

I finally settled on an impressive slate of 20 beers and 14 whiskies, representing respectively eight brewing nations and all the major whisky-producing areas of Scotland, save the small southwestern region of Campbeltown, which was only omitted because I could not get my hands on any such malts. To help me in the tasting, I relied on the very enthusiastic assistance of two friends, Alastair Hood and Geoff Tomlinson, neither of whom was a specialized taster but who both shared my enthusiasm for great beer and whisky. My thinking behind their selection was to enlist the opinions of beer and whisky lovers rather than experts and, as it turned out, it was a decision wisely made.

After a brief explanation of the evening's goal, we set about experimenting, nosing the beers and whiskies first and then sipping the most likely partners. With 280 possible pairs on the table, caution and pace were of the utmost importance.

Two rules of thumb quickly became obvious as we proceeded in our pursuit of the perfect pair, and both stemmed from ideas I had earlier proposed. For starters, it was blatantly apparent that none of the lagers on the table were going to work with any of the whiskies. Not that it was surprising to find that neither of the German or Bohemian pilsners was suited to whisky accompaniment, but it did come as a bit of a shock to find that, even at 6% alcohol by volume, the excellent Rebellion malt liquor from Upper Canada Brewing was drowned by the flavor of the mildest of Lowland malts.

The subsequent revelation, which came as a bit of a surprise despite my earlier research with hoppy beers, was that the beer would have to contain a significant amount of sweetness if the pairing was going to work. This tenet, roundly agreed upon at the table, eliminated some otherwise excellent beers such as Orval Trappist and Sierra Nevada Stout, brands I had previously suspected would make it to the final round. In the end, the driest beer to make it to a partnership was Pike Place Pale Ale, and even that was only with the light and delicate Lowland malt, Littlemill.

The most obvious match of the night — the extremely peaty Lagavulin from Islay with the world-classic rauchbier from the German brewery Schlenkerla — turned out to be almost too much for my guest tasters, although I personally found it to be quite enjoyable. The intensity of the smoky flavors contained in both beverages prompted the tongue-in-cheek suggestion of trying the two drinks while smoking a cigar and sitting around a camp fire!

As the evening wore on, we found that the most compatible pairs — the "matches made in heaven" — used whiskies from the upper end of the flavor-potency scale: those more assertive than the Speysides yet mellower than the Islays. As for the beers, apart from a few notable exceptions, consensus favored a strongly malty character, relatively low hopping and a higher than average alcohol content. And as might be expected, the Scotch ales involved in the tasting scored well beside more than a couple of whiskies.

In the end, we concluded that the finest matches of the night were the marvelous McEwan's Scotch Ale from Scotland paired with the 12-year-old malt from that country's northernmost distiller, Highland Park, and the Belgian export Corsendonk Pale Ale matched to the 14-year-old west Highlander from Oban. Runners-up included the aforementioned Pike Place Pale Ale (as contract-brewed by Catamount) married to the subtle, eight-year-old Lowland malt from Littlemill and the silken St. Ambroise Oatmeal Stout mated with the ten-year-old Skye malt from Talisker. All in all, it was indeed an evening to remember, particularly when next ordering a pint with a dram on the side.

AT THE MOVIES

I know of at least one city in North America where you can order your beer from the bar "to go" (New Orleans), I have heard of a Major League ballpark where you can select from dozens of local and imported brews at "Beers of the World" booths (Veterans Stadium in Philadelphia) and I have been to outdoor music festivals in Chicago where private vendors push shopping carts full of beer through the crowds, but I know of no place on this continent where you can buy beer at the movies.

It is an odd situation, really. You can walk into any theater in the land and order up a bucket of soda pop large enough to bathe in, but you cannot buy a beer to take to your seat. Sure, I understand the concern about the diuretic effect of beer and the possible consequences thereof, but are we really expected to believe that a 12-ounce beer would make one have to pee more than a giga-ounce pail of pop would? Or is it just that we are still too uptight about drinking in North America to allow such a heretical act as drinking beer at the "moving pictures"? Methinks it just might be the latter.

As one who does not care for soda and is far too cheap to spend five bucks on a cup of water with carbon dioxide injected into it, I have spent many a thirsty hour at the movies pondering the reason that I cannot enjoy a glass of beer, especially when Cindy Lou down the aisle can have her pick of Coke, ginger ale, Sprite, lemon, kiwi and lime drink, artificially sweetened and decaffeinated iced tea, double decaffeinated latte and four brands of mineral water. And because theaters are notoriously dry even when it's raining cats and dogs outdoors, my first act upon leaving the cinema is usually to stop at the nearest water fountain and dominate it for about five minutes. As the song says, it makes me wonder.

It is not just my thirst that makes me think movies would be better if they could be enjoyed with a glass of beer; it is my imagination, as well. Because like almost everything else on the face of the planet, I think that movies could be adeptly partnered with appropriate beers.

It is a fascinating concept, to be sure, and one that brings certain pairs immediately to mind. One partnership, for example, would have to be the black-and-white classic *Casablanca* matched with the complex, dry Trois de Pique bock from Quebec City's L'Inox, with its whiskyish body paying homage to the drink of choice at Rick's Café Américain. Another match that would appear obvious (to me, at least) is that of Orson Welles's masterpiece, *Citizen Kane,* married to the Icicle Creek Winter Ale from Portland Brewing, a fine, rich beer with a note of rosy florals — dare I say a rosebud of taste? — in its body.

Of course, homages and thinly veiled references are not the only way to match movies to beers. For example, what filmed chronicle of early American history would not improve with the addition of a glass of Dock Street's Thomas Jefferson's Ale, purportedly brewed from the original recipe favored by that founding father? And who could help but match the syrupy Christmas cheer of *It's a Wonderful Life* with the sweet maple flavors of Niagara Falls Maple Wheat? For any of the great spaghetti westerns made by Sergio Leone and Clint Eastwood, a peppery Mexicali Rogue from Oregon's Rogue Brewing would certainly seem right, or perhaps it should be an oregano-seasoned Birra Perfeto from the Pike Place Brewery in Seattle, instead.

Moving on to some slightly more modern films, a Pabst Blue Ribbon might seem like the obvious choice for David Lynch's dark masterpiece, *Blue Velvet,* but I'm not Dennis Hopper and I think that a Black Velvet might be more to my palate, perhaps made with Veuve Clicquot and the Hardy Stout from Ontario's Hart Brewing. While I have yet to see the blockbuster *Jurassic Park,* I would have to imagine that the Ichthyosaur Pale Ale from Nevada's Great Basin Brewing Company would be appropriate, and it is something else I have yet to experience. For *Forrest Gump,* whose mother always told him that life was like a box of chocolates, the logical brew would have to be the Brooklyn Brewery's exemplary Black Chocolate Stout, a beer that does not actually contain chocolate and therefore proves the rest of Forrest's mom's adage: that you never know what you're gonna get.

The pairings could conceivably continue *ad infinitum.* For as long as Hollywood continues to crank out films and North America's micros keep on turning out new beers, there will always be more than adequate numbers of each to keep the marriages vibrant. Just as long as no eager brewer ever tries to come up with a beer that will match Francis Ford Coppola's epic odyssey, *Apocalypse Now*!

SMOKING BEERS

I am not a cigar smoker.

I mention this by way of putting my next beer-matching expedition into some kind of perspective, because the excursion in question was part of a rather peculiar and twofold quest. The subject, as you may have guessed, was to be cigars and the dual purposes were to find out more about cigars than I could cull from the pages of *Cigar Aficionado* and, if possible, figure out the basis for the recent revival of cigar appreciation, and then to see if I could find a beer that would match the power of a reasonably fine Cuban cigar. Such big plans for a small cigar!

When I first began this journey in earnest, I had no writing assignment in mind and my focus was purely exploratory. As the process developed, however, I knew that I was on to something and quickly snagged the interest of Bill Owens, the publisher of *Beer: the Magazine*. Thoughts were exchanged, a deal was struck and my smoky adventures began.

The first step was to visit Toronto's Havana House, a reputable and respected cigar merchant. As soon as I set foot in the plush confines of the store, I knew that I had entered an environment that was all too foreign to me. An almost library-like air of reverence hung over the shop and the leafy aromas of so many tobaccos perfumed the atmosphere, giving it a heady and slightly narcotic scent. I could not have felt more the outsider if I had been standing dressed in a polar suit on the banks of the Nile in midday.

I informed the proprietor of the store about the details of my mission and she led me into the glass-enclosed, climate-controlled humidor room at the back of the small shop. Recognizing that I likely did not wish to shell out 20 dollars or more for something I may not be able to appreciate, my kind guide directed me to a five-dollar Ramon Allones from Cuba. Thus armed with my cigar, I then faced the challenge of deciding the circumstances under which I would effect my smoking experiment.

Instinctively, I knew that I could immediately rule out any and all pilsners from contention in this pairing. No matter how well hopped, there was no way I could envision a pale beer holding up to the strong, leafy smoke of a cigar. Similarly, I also eliminated wheat beers of all stripes, mild ales, Vienna lagers and dunkels from participation in my experiment, confident that their ranks would yield no match for the mighty Cuban.

Even with all those exceptions, however, I was still left with a significant supply of beer styles from which to choose, and only a limited amount of cigar! With a situation such as this, I knew that the effort was going to require the testing of several brews over the course of two or three days and so I decided that I would have to rely on a practice I have since found to be heretical in cigar-smoking circles: I would need to clip the cigar after each session.

The first brew to take a crack at my cigar was Upper Canada Dark Ale, a somewhat variable ale brewed broadly in the British tradition with a walnutty body holding notes of caramel and berry. Because the ale is dryish and of medium strength (5% alcohol by volume), I thought that it might be able to complement the cigar without detracting from its smoke with an excessive amount of fruit or sugar. Unfortunately, I was dead wrong in my assumption and the cigar so dominated the ale that I might as well have been imbibing iced tea for all that I could taste. Something stronger was definitely going to be in order for this cigar.

As I worked through the next few tastings, I noted that, for some reason, I was singularly unable to pin down the complementary needs of the cigar. I tried a strong, Irish-style ale from Big Rock, McNally's Extra Ale, and found it to be strong enough to match the cigar but so contrasting in taste that the two flavors virtually battled it out for supremacy on my palate. I then opted for a cherry-flavored brown ale from Belgium, the outstanding Liefmans Kriek, and discovered that its intense flavors were actually too much for the comparatively mild-tasting Cuban. Seldom had I experienced such difficulties in trying to make a flavor pairing.

Finally, realizing that my best bet would likely lie in the realm of porters and stouts, I tried both a dry and a sweet stout with my now-dwindling Cuban. My premise for this last-ditch attempt lay in the smokiness of the black malts that give stouts their roasty and sometimes burnt characters and black colors. In the flavor and aroma traits that these malts provide, I hoped to find some that would set off the taste of the cigar.

Pairing a classic dry stout with an equally classic Cuban cigar seemed like a great idea at the time and were I to have done so at the start of the smoke, it might have been an admirable success. As the flame curled toward the cigar band, however, the flavor of the Cuban had become too strong to be supported by the relatively tender character of the Guinness. My last chance lay in the sweet, plummy and almost refreshing character of Jamaica's Dragon Stout.

I have always been a staunch defender of the strong, sweet stouts of the Caribbean, and given that the dry stout missed by only a whisker, I hoped that the Dragon might provide what the Irish classic lacked. What I was expecting was that the lighter but more vibrant body of the Dragon, coupled with its cellar temperature and slight smokiness, would balance nicely the hot intensity of the nearly finished cigar, and I was finally right.

Taking the final few puffs from my stub of a cigar, I mused upon appropriateness of my final pairing. In retrospect, I suppose that I should have known at the outset to look to a Caribbean beer for a complement to a Caribbean cigar.

I have not repeated my cigar experiment since those days in the summer of 1993 and I somehow doubt that I ever will. For although I more or less enjoyed the Cuban cigar and certainly had an entertaining time in pursuit of a complementary beer, I do not think that I truly appreciated the cigar the way it deserved to be appreciated. If I read my *Cigar Aficionado* correctly, there should be much more to a good cigar than the casual and almost incidental pleasures I felt during my smoky quest, so perhaps future adventures would best be left to genuine cigar smokers. Any takers?

AND NOW IT'S YOUR TURN

Over the course of this book, I have presented many ideas about this most favored beverage we know as beer. Some of my thoughts have been simple reiterations of concepts that have been around for years and others are new and, I hope, unique takes on the hundreds of fascinating brews now available to North Americans. I have passed from relatively mundane suggestions about how best to get to know this nascent industry known as microbrewing to some whimsical notions about matching beer styles and labels to music and movies. And I only hope that reading them has been as much fun for you as writing them was for me.

You will not agree with all of my thoughts and conjectures and neither should you. Taste is a very personal concept, both in its literal definition and its figurative one, and I certainly did not write this book in an attempt to convince readers that oysters should *always* be enjoyed with stout or that the beautiful, falsetto vocals of Aaron Neville *may only* be fully appreciated when accompanied by a glass of Belle Gueulle. These suggestions are meant only as starting blocks for your own beery explorations, and where you go from here is entirely up to you.

I have mentioned many beers by name in the preceding pages and the best of them are listed by brewery in Appendix I, but these, too, are offered only as places from which to begin. There are hundreds of breweries and beers on the North American market with new ones appearing every day, and no single person could possibly claim to have recommended *all* of the greats. My advice, as repeated several times throughout this book, is to taste for yourself what is available and make your own assessments, because, after all, you have the only opinion that you have to answer to.

Beyond the beer and the beer appreciation, however, there is another message that I have tried to convey. That message, a clarion call of sorts, is a cry to reclaim the enjoyment that already exists so plainly and simply in our lives. Whether it is the comfort of a good beer sipped among friends, the rapturous taste of a piece of fruit picked at perfect ripeness or the emotional high brought on by an uplifting piece of music, such pleasures are easily found if we only allow ourselves to take note of them. And they can contribute so much to the quality of our lives.

So let me now encourage you to go forth with a renewed purpose in your life: to relish it rather than just live it. And if that enjoyment involves beer hunts and other beer-tasting pursuits, so much the better, because you have a great big field on which to play. North America now has one of the largest and most vibrant craft-brewing industries in the world, and it is all yours just for the asking.

As tempting as it is to close this book by asking you to mail in your thoughts on what makes for great beer enjoyment or what components you involve in your favorite beer match, I am not going to take the bait. Because even though I am always pleased to hear from readers through the offices of my publisher, I also believe wholeheartedly that beer enjoyment is a most personal thing and that the only ones who need benefit from your thoughts on the subject are those people with whom you specifically choose to share your experiences.

Instead, then, I will finish by encouraging you to examine, experiment with and, most of all, explore the fascinating and diverse world of beer and brewing. And to do so with respect — for yourself, for others and for this drinkable work of art we call beer.

APPENDIX I

THE BEERS OF THE BOOK

The following list includes only those North American beers and breweries that are mentioned at some point in *A Taste For Beer* and recommmended by the author. It is by no means to be considered a complete listing of the best beers on the continent and is provided only to assist readers in tracking down specific beers which, for one reason or another, may have stimulated their interest. Because that is part of what beer enjoyment is all about.

Adler Brau/Appleton
Brewing Company
1004 Olde Oneida Street, Appleton,
WI 54915
Pumpkin Spice Beer

Alaskan Brewing Company
5429 Shaune Drive, Juneau, AK
99801
Alaskan Smoked Porter

Algonquin Brewing Company
1270 Central Parkway West,
Mississauga, ON L5C 4P4
Special Reserve Ale

Anchor Brewing Company
1705 Mariposa Street,
San Francisco, CA 94107
Old Foghorn Barley Wine, Anchor Wheat Ale, Our Special Ale, Anchor Steam Beer, Liberty Ale, Ninkasi

Anderson Valley Brewing Company
P.O. Box 505 (14081 Highway 128), Boonville, CA 95415
Barney Flats Oatmeal Stout

**Arctic Brewing Company/
Bush Pilot Brewpub**
3502 Wiley Road, Yellowknife,
N.W.T. X1A 2L5

August Schell
P.O. Box 580414, Minneapolis, MN
55458-0414
August Schell Pils

Big Rock Brewing
6403 35th Street S.E. Calgary, AB
T2E 1N2
Grasshopper Wheat Ale, Buzzard Breath Ale, Traditional Ale, McNally's Extra Irish Ale

Bohannon Brewing Company
134 Second Avenue North,
Nashville, TN 37201
Market Street Wheat Beer

Boston Beer Company
30 Germania Street, Boston,
MA 02130
Samuel Adams Cranberry Lambic, Samuel Adams Double Bock,

Samuel Adams Dunkel Weizen,
Samuel Adams Triple Bock,
Samuel Adams Winter Lager,
Samuel Adams Boston Lager

Brasal–Brasserie Allemande
8477 Rue Cordner, Lasalle,
(Montreal), QC H8N 2X2
Brasal Bock, Hopps Bräu, Spécial

Brasseurs du Nord
18 Kennedy, St. Jérôme,
QC J7Y 4B4
Boréale Rousse

Brick Brewing Company
181 King Street S., Waterloo,
ON N2J 1P7
Anniversary Bock, Premium Lager

Brooklyn Brewery
118 North 11th Street, Brooklyn,
NY 11211
Black Chocolate Stout,
Brooklyn Brown Ale

Buffalo Bill's Brewery
Box 510, Hayward, CA 94543-0510
Buffalo Bill's Pumpkin Ale

Capital Brewery Company
7734 Terrace Avenue, Middleton,
WI 53560
Garten Bräu Bock

Carib Brewery
Eastern Main Road, Champs Fleurs,
Trinidad, West Indies
Carib Royal Stout

Catamount Brewing Company
58 South Main Street, P.O. Box
457, White River Junction, VT 05001

Catamount Gold, Catamount
Christmas Ale, Oktoberfest,
Catamount Porter

Celis Brewery
2431 Forbes Drive, Austin,
TX 78754
Celis White, Celis Grand Cru

Conners Brewery
17C Isabella Street, Toronto,
ON M4Y 1M7
Conners Best Bitter, Conners Ale

Chicago Brewing Company
1830 N. Besly Court, Chicago,
IL 60622
Big Shoulders Porter

Creemore Springs Brewery Limited
Box 369, 139 Mill Street, Creemore,
ON L0M 1G0
Creemore Springs Premium Lager

Crescent City Brewhouse
527 Decatur Street, New Orleans,
LA 70130
Black Forest Dunkel,
Crescent City Pilsner

Denison's Brewing Co.
75 Victoria Street, Toronto,
ON M5C 2B1
Weizen

Deschutes Brewery
901 S.W. Simpson Avenue, Bend,
OR 97702
Black Butte Porter

Desnoes & Geddes
214 Spanish Town Road, P.O. Box
190, Kingston 11, Jamaica
Dragon Stout

D. L. Geary Brewing Company
38 Evergreen Drive, Portland,
ME 04103
Geary's Special Hampshire Ale

Dock Street Brewing Company
2 Logan Square, Philadelphia,
PA 19103
Thomas Jefferson's Ale

Drummond Brewing,
2210 Gaetz Avenue, Red Deer, AB
T4R 1W5
Wolfsbrau Amber Lager

FEMSA Cerveza
Avenue Alfonso Reyes 2202 NTE.,
Monterrey, N.L., Mexico,
C.P. 64442
Dos Equis, Bohemia

Frankenmuth Brewery
425 South Main Street,
Frankenmuth, MI 48734
Frankenmuth Dark,
Frankenmuth Bock

Les Brasseurs GMT
5710 Garnier Street, Montréal, QC
H2G 2Z7
Belle Gueulle

Goose Island Brewing Company
1800 North Clybourn, Chicago,
IL 60614
Kölsch, Clybourn Porter

Gordon Biersch Brewery
Restaurant
2 Harrison Street, San Francisco,
CA 94120 (Also San Jose, CA,
Palo Alto, CA, Pasadena, CA and
Honolulu, HI)

Granite Brewery
245 Eglinton Avenue East, Toronto,
ON M4P 3B7
Best Bitter

Granite Brewery
1222 Barrington Street, Halifax,
NS B3J 1Y4

Granville Island Brewing
1441 Cartwright St., Granville
Island, Vancouver, BC V6H 3R7
10th Anniversary Ale,
Island Bock

Gray's Brewing Company
2424 W. Court Street, Janesville,
WI 53545
Gray's Classic Oatmeal Stout

Great Divide Brewing Company
2201 Arapahoe Street, Denver,
CO 80205
Arapahoe Amber Ale

Hart Breweries
175 Industrial Ave., Carleton Place,
ON K7C 3V7
Hart Amber Ale, Festive Brown Ale,
Dragon's Breath Pale Ale,
Hardy Stout

Hart Brewing
110 W. Marine Drive, Kalama,
WA 98625
Pyramid Apricot Ale, Pyramid
Wheaten Bock, Pyramid Pale Ale

Heckler Brewing Compaany
P.O. Box 947, Tahoe City, CA
96145
Heckler Bräu Fest Märzen,
Dopple Bock

Holy Cow! Casino, Cafe and Brewery
2423 Las Vegas Boulevard So.,
Las Vegas, NV 89104
Holy Cow! Pale Ale

Hudepohl-Schoenling
1625 Central Parkway, Cincinnati,
OH 45214
Little Kings Cream Ale

L'Inox Maîtres Brasseurs
37 St-André Street, Vieux-Port de
Québec, QC G1K 8T3
Trois de Pique

Kennebunkport Brewing Company
8 Western Avenue #6, Kennebunk,
ME 04043
Blue Fin Stout

Kessler Brewery
1439 Harris Street, Helena,
MT 59601
Kessler Doppelbock

Labatt Breweries of Canada
Labatt House, BCE Place,
181 Bay Street, Suite 200,
P.O. Box 786, Toronto,
ON M5J 2T3
John Labatt Classic Wheat

Lakefront Brewery
818A East Chambers Street,
Milwaukee, WI 53212
Lakefront Weisse, Pumpkin Lager

Marin Brewing Company
1809 Larkspur Landing Circle,
Larkspur, CA 94939
Bluebeery Ale,
Raspberry Trail Ale,
Stinson Beach Peach

Brasserie McAuslan
4850 St. Ambroise, Bureau 100,
Montréal, QC H4C 3N8
St. Ambroise Oatmeal Stout,
St. Ambroise Pale Ale

Mendocino Brewing Company
13351 South Highway 101 S.,
P.O. Box 400, Hopland, CA 95449
Red Tail Ale

Miller Brewing Company
3939 West Highland Boulevard,
Milwaukee, WI 53201-0482
Reserve Velvet Stout

Molson Breweries
175 Bloor Street East, North Tower,
Toronto, ON M4W 3S4
Stock Ale, Signature Series
Amber Lager

New Belgium Brewing Company
350 Linden Street, Ft. Collins,
CO 80524
Abbey Trappist Style Ale

New Glarus Brewing Company
County Road W., Highway 69,
P.O. Box 328, New Glarus, WI
53574-0328
New Glarus Belgian Red, Uff-da Bock

Niagara Falls Brewing Company
6863 Lundy's Lane, Niagara Falls,
ON L2G 1V7
Eisbock, Olde Jack Strong Ale,
Maple Wheat, Gritstone Ale,
Brock's Extra Stout

**Norwich Inn/Jasper Murdock's
Alehouse**
P.O. Box 908, Main Street,
Norwich, VT 05055

Okanagan Spring Brewery
3535 Foster Avenue,
Vancouver, BC V5R 4X3
Olde English Porter,
Old Munich Wheat

Oregon Ale and Beer Company
5875 SW Lakeview Boulevard,
Lake Oswego, OR 97035
Oregon Nut Brown Ale

Pete's Brewing Company
514 High Street, Palo Alto,
CA 94301
Pete's Wicked Winter Brew,
Pete's Wicked Ale

Pike Place Brewery
1432 Western Avenue, Seattle,
WA 98101
Pike Place Pale Ale,
Birra Perfeto

Portland Brewing Company
1339 N.W. Flanders Street,
Portland, OR 9720
McTarnahans Ale,
Icicle Creek Winter Ale

The Redhook Ale Brewery
3400 Phinney Avenue North,
Seattle, WA 98103
Blackhook Porter, Winterhook,
Wheathook

Rogue Ales
2320 OSU Drive, Newport,
OR 97365
Doppel Mogul,
Mogul Ale, Rogue Smoke,
Old Crustacean Barley Wine,
Shakespeare Stout, Mo Ale,
Mexicali Rogue

Santa Fe Brewing Company
HC-75 Box 83, Galisteo,
NM 87540
Sangre de Frambuesa

Sierra Nevada Brewing Company
1075 E. 20th Street, Chico,
CA 95928
Sierra Nevada Pale Ale, Sierra
Nevada Stout, Sierra Nevada Pale
Bock, Bigfoot Barley Wine,
Celebration Ale

Sleeman Brewing and Malting
Company
551 Clair Road West, Guelph, ON
N1H 6H9
Sleeman Cream Ale

Spinnakers Brewing
308 Catherine Street, Victoria, BC
V9A 3S8

Spring Street Brewing Company
60 Spring Street, New York,
NY 10012
Amber Wit, Wit

Stoudt's Brewing Company
P.O. Box 880, Rt. 272, Adamstown,
PA 19501
Stoudt Pilsener, Bock,
Honey Double Mai-Bock,
Double Bock, Holiday Bock, Fest

St. Stan's Brewing Company
821 L Street, Modesto, CA 95354
St. Stan's Amber Alt

Swan's Pub/
Buckerfield Brewery
506 Pandora Street, Victoria, BC
V8W 1N6

Tabernash Brewing Company
205 Denargo Market, Denver,
CO 80216
Tabernash Weiss

Taylor & Bate Brewery
55 Mill Street West, Elora, ON
N0B 1S0
Elora Grand Porter

Thomas Kemper Brewing Company
22381 Foss Road NE, Poulsbo,
WA 98370
Integrale

Triple Rock Brewery & Alehouse
1920 Shattuck Avenue, Berkeley,
CA 94704

Twenty Tank Brewery
316 11th Street, San Francisco,
CA 94103

Unibroue, 80 Des Carrieres
Chambly, QC G3L 2H6
*Fin du Monde, Blanche de Chambly,
Maudite*

Upper Canada Brewing Company
2 Atlantic Avenue, Toronto, ON
M6K 1X8
*Rebellion, Upper Canada Lager,
Dark Ale*

Vancouver Island Brewing
24–6809 Kirkpatrick Cr., R.R. #3,
Victoria, BC V8X 3X1
*Hermann's Dark Lager,
Hermannator Bock*

The Vermont Pub & Brewery
144 College Street, Burlington,
VT 05401
Wee Heavy, Dogbite Bitter

Wellington County Brewer
950 Woodlawn Rd., Guelph, ON
N1K 1B8
Imperial Stout, Arkell Best Bitter

Whistler Brewing Co.
1209 Alpha Lake Road, Whistler,
BC V0N 1B1
*Whistler Premium Lager, Whistler's
Mother Pale Ale, Black Tusk Ale*

Widmer Brewing Company
929 North Russell Street, Portland,
OR 97227
Widmer Hefe-Weizen

Wild Boar Brewing Company
P.O. Box 8239, Atlanta, GA 30306
Wild Boar Amber

William & Scott Co.
8460 Higuera Street, Culver City,
CA 90232
*Rhino Chasers Winterful,
Rhino Chasers American Ale,
Rhino Chasers Amber Ale,
Rhino Chasers Därk Lager*

Wynkoop Brewing Company
1634 Eighteenth Street, Denver,
CO 80202
Wynkoop ESB

Zip City Brewing Company
3 West 18th Street, New York,
NY 10011
*Zip City Rauchbier,
Zip City Kölsch*

APPENDIX II

REFERENCES

REFERENCE BOOKS

The extensive listing below is composed of books that have in some way contributed to the creation of this book. In certain instances, these have been referenced directly while, on other occasions, they may have provided some form of subconscious stimulation on a particular topic. Without exception, however, each book is enthusiastically recommended.

Cooking

Aidells, Bruce and Denis Kelly, *Real Beer and Good Eats*. Alfred A. Knopf, New York, 1993.

Lukins, Sheila, *All Around the World Cookbook*. Workman Publishing, New York, 1994.

Schermerhorn, Candy, *Great American Beer Cookbook*. Brewers Publications, Boulder, CO, 1994.

Food

Fiorito, Joe, *Comfort Me with Apples*. NuAge Editions, Montreal, 1994.

Fisher, M.F.K., *The Art of Eating*. Collier Books, New York, 1990.

Jacobs, Jay, *A Glutton for Punishment*. Atlantic Monthly Press, New York, 1990.

MacClancy, Jeremy, *Consuming Culture*. Chapmans Publishers, London, 1992.

McGee, Harold, *On Food and Cooking*. Collier Books, New York, 1984.

Guides

Beaumont, Stephen, *Great Canadian Beer Guide*. Macmillan Canada, Toronto, 1994.

Erickson, Jack, *Brewery Adventures in the Big East*. Red Brick Press, Sonoma, CA, 1993.

Erickson, Jack, *California Brewin'*. Red Brick Press, Sonoma, CA, 1993.

Finch, Christopher, *A Connoisseur's Guide to the World's Best Beer*. Abbeville Press, New York, 1989.

Finch, Christopher, & W. Scott Griffiths, *America's Best Beers*. Little, Brown and Company, Boston, 1994.

Jackson, Michael, *The Simon & Schuster Pocket Guide to Beer*. Simon & Schuster Inc., New York, 1994.

Jackson, Michael, *The New World Guide to Beer*. Running Press, Philadelphia, 1988.

Johnson, Steve, *On Tap: Guide to North American Brewpubs*. WBR Publications, Clemson, SC, 1994.

Johnson, Steve, *On Tap New England*. WBR Publications, Clemson, SC, 1994.

MacKinnon, Jamie, *The Ontario Beer Guide*. Riverwood Publishers, Sharon, Ontario, 1992.

Nachel, Marty, *Beer Across America: A Regional Guide to Brewpubs and Microbreweries*. Storey Publishing, Pownal, VT, 1995.

Wood, Heather, *The Beer Directory: An International Guide*. Storey Publishing, Pownal, VT, 1995.

Homebrewing

Lutzen, Karl F., & Mark Stevens, *Homebrew Favorites: A Coast-to-Coast Collection of More Than 240 Beer and Ale Recipes*. Storey Publishing, Pownal, VT, 1994.

Miller, Dave, *Brewing the World's Great Beers: A Step-by-Step Guide*. Storey Publishing, Pownal, VT, 1992.

Miller, Dave, *Dave Miller's Homebrewing Guide: Everything You Need to Know to Make Great-Tasting Beer*. Storey Publishing, Pownal, VT, 1995.

Papazian, Charlie, *The Home Brewer's Companion*. Avon Books, New York, 1994.

Papazian, Charlie, *The New Complete Guide to Home Brewing*. Avon Books, New York, 1991.

Reese, M.R., *Better Beer & How to Brew It*. Garden Way Publishing, Pownal, VT, 1978.

Style

D'Eer, Mario, *Le Guide de la Bonne Bière*. Editions du Trécarré, Ville Saint Laurent, Québec, 1989. (Published in french.)

Eckhardt, Fred, *The Essentials of Beer Style*. Fred Eckhardt Communications, Portland, OR, 1989.

Fix, George, & Laurie, *Vienna, Märzen, Oktoberfest*. Brewers Publications, Boulder, CO, 1991.

Forget, Carl, *Dictionary of Beer and Brewing*. Brewers Publications, Boulder, CO, 1988.

Foster, Terry, *Pale Ale*. Brewers Publications, Boulder, CO, 1990.

Foster, Terry, *Porter*. Brewers Publications, Boulder, CO, 1992.

Guinard, Jean-Xavier, *Lambic*. Brewers Publications, Boulder, CO, 1990.

Jackson, Michael, *Michael Jackson's Beer Companion*. Running Press, Philadelphia, 1993.

Miller, David, *Continental Pilsener*. Brewers Publications, Boulder, CO, 1990.

Noonan, Gregory, *Scotch Ale*. Brewers Publications, Boulder, CO, 1993.

Rajotte, Pierre, *Belgian Ale*. Brewers Publications, Boulder, CO, 1992.

Richman, Darryl, *Bock*. Brewers Publications, Boulder, CO, 1994.

Smith, Gregg, *The Beer Enthusiast's Guide*. Storey Publishing, Pownal, VT, 1994.

Warner, Eric, *German Wheat Beer*. Brewers Publications, Boulder, CO, 1992.

PERIODICALS

Beer journalism is a growth industry, and there are new publications entering the North American market on a seemingly continual basis. The following list — compiled with the assistance of *The Celebrator Beer News* — is as complete as possible at the time of writing.

Magazines

All About Beer, 1627 Marion Ave., Durham, NC, USA 27705.

American Brewer, Box 510, Hayward, CA, USA 94543-0510.

Beer Magazine, 102 Burlington Cr., Ottawa, ON, Canada K1T 3K5.

Beer: The Magazine, Box 717, Hayward, CA, USA 94543-0717.

BièreMAG, 102 Burlington Cr., Ottawa, ON, Canada K1T 3K5. (Published in french.)

Healthy Drinking, 4714 N.E. 50th St., Seattle, WA, USA 98105-2908.

Juice, P.O. Box 9068, Berkeley, CA, USA 94709.

The Malt Advocate, 3416 Oak Hill Rd., Emmaus, PA, USA 18049.

Matter World Times, P.O. Box 275, White Plains, NY, USA 10602. (Newsletter.)

Northwest Brew News, 22833 Bothell-Everett Hwy. Ste. 1139, Bothell, WA, USA 98021-9365. (Newsletter.)

On Tap: The Newsletter, P.O. Box 71, Clemson, SC, USA 29633.

The Pint Post, 12345 Lake City Way NE #159, Seattle, WA, USA 98125.

What's On Tap, P.O. Box 7779, Berkeley, CA, USA 94709-7779.

Brewspapers

Ale Street News, P.O. Box 1125, Maywood, NJ, USA 07607.

Barleycorn, P.O. Box 2328, Falls Church, VA, USA 22042.

Beer & Tavern Chronicle, 244 Madison Ave., Suite 164, New York, NY, USA 10016.

Brew Hawaii, 41–610 Nonokio St., Waimanolo, HI, USA 96795.

The Celebrator Beer News, P.O. Box 375, Hayward, CA, USA 94543.

Midwest Beer Notes, 339 6th Ave., Clayton, WI, USA 54004.

Rocky Mountain Brews, 251 Jefferson, Fort Collins, CO, USA 80524.

Southern Draft Brew News, 702 Sailfish Rd., Winter Springs, FL, USA 32708.

Southwest Brewing News, 11405 Evening Star Dr., Austin, TX, USA 78739.

What's Brewing, P.O. Box 30101, Saanich Centre Postal Outlet, Victoria, BC, Canada V8X 5E1. (Not the U.K. paper of the same name.)

Yankee Brew News, P.O. Box 8053, JFK Station, Boston, MA, USA 02114.